PRAISE F

Georgia Nagel is known as the "pet sitter," but she is so much more than that. Her intuitive ability to hone in on what you or your pet needs is awesome, as is her kind and gentle heart. Georgia can give you practical and spiritual insight you otherwise would never know. Her gifts are many and can change your life and your pet's. I highly recommend Georgia's services.

—**Sunny Dawn Johnston**- author of, *Invoking the Archangels*, *The Love Never Ends* and *Detox Your Life*

"As an avid animal lover, I've been looking for a book like Pet Talker for several years. So imagine my delight when I sat down to read Pet Talker and found it was not only packed full of heartfelt stories of Georgia's experiences as a pet sitter and animal communicator, but it also offers tips and tools I can implement with my own animals to learn to develop my intuition and communicate more effectively.

This book will take you on a journey—you'll laugh, you'll cry, and in the end you'll have discovered valuable insights and communication techniques. Georgia Nagel is a gifted animal intuitive and healer, and it's clear her life's purpose is to give these animals a voice and teach others about their special place in our world. I firmly believe that by learning to understand what animals are here to teach us and how to better understand their needs can only benefit us all, and Georgia shares all that and more with us in Pet Talker."

—**Shanda Trofe**, publisher & author coach, bestselling author of *Write from the Heart* and *Authorpreneur*

"I have known Georgia for years and to see her engage with animals and put her whole heart into communicating with them has been a gift.

My cat Charlie had not been eating and I could see his neck was not right. I asked Georgia to please learn what was needed to assist him.

When Georgia tuned into him she started to laugh and said he told her that he had his neck stretched. Georgia had no idea that I had taken him to the vet or the chiropractor.

It gave me such validation that the information she receives is coming from our pets.

I told our pet chiropractor about the feedback and he said, "WOW, tell her she is a clear channel."

Georgia was also able to offer me a glimpse of Charlie in a past life we shared. She described his looks and when I sent a picture she responded, "OMG, that's Charlie, except in the past life he was black and white."

Georgia is the real deal, my friends, and always looks out for your fuzzy loved ones."

—**Jodie Harvala,** author of *The Magic of Space Clearing* and *ABC's of Intuition* and creator of The Spirit School.

"There may not be a word in our vocabulary that describes what Georgia does in her work with animals. From a young age, she has enjoyed a connection with animals that has only deepened with time. It is a rare person who can be accomplished in both the physical and intuitive spheres, and that describes Georgia. I have witnessed her connection, communication and understanding with animals. Read this book and share that experience. "

—Nancy Nereson

*Deb!
Thank you for being the cat lover, and your great energy!
Georgia Nagel*

PET TALKER

LISTENING TO THOSE WHO SPEAK SILENTLY

GEORGIA NAGEL

PET TALKER
LISTENING TO THOSE WHO SPEAK SILENTLY

by GEORGIA NAGEL

Copyright © 2017. Georgia Nagel. All Rights Reserved. No part of this publication may be reproduced, distributed, or transmitted in any form or by any means, including photocopying, recording, or other electronic or mechanical methods, without the prior written permission of the publisher, except in the case of brief quotations embodied in critical reviews and certain other noncommercial uses permitted by copyright law.

Published by
Transcendent Publishing
P.O. Box 66202
St. Pete Beach, FL 33736
www.transcendentpublishing.com

Transcendent
Publishing

Cover and author photograph: Stacy Chesley
Little Red Shack Photography

ISBN-10: 0-9987576-9-1
ISBN-13: 978-0-9987576-9-8
Library of Congress Control Number: 2017946852

Printed in the United States of America.

To my dogs—Shooz and Midnite—who taught me that I have intuitive abilities and how to use them. Although they are no longer in this physical world, they are still teaching me every day the unconditional love of the creatures of this earth.
I Love You, Boys!!!

CONTENTS

FOREWORD BY MELISSA KIM CORTER i

INTRODUCTION v

CHAPTER ONE: A LIFE-CHANGING DAY 1

CHAPTER TWO: MY BEGINNING WITH ANIMALS 11

CHAPTER THREE: LISTEN TO THE BIG DOGS 19

CHAPTER FOUR: LITTLE DOGS, BIG VOICES 29

CHAPTER FIVE: I JUST KNOW 35

CHAPTER SIX: THE CAT'S MEOW 45

CHAPTER SEVEN: FINDING THE LOST 55

CHAPTER EIGHT: END OF LIFE WITH YOUR PET 71

CHAPTER NINE: MAYOR DUKE 93

CHAPTER TEN: INTUITIVE READINGS 97

CHAPTER ELEVEN: RECLAIMING YOUR INTUITIVE SKILLS 107

CHAPTER TWELVE: TOOLS 117

CHAPTER THIRTEEN: SHALL WE TRY? 127

CHAPTER FOURTEEN: IN CLOSING 131

PET GALLERY 135

ABOUT THE AUTHOR 149

ACKNOWLEDGMENTS 151

TESTIMONIALS 153

WORK WITH GEORGIA 157

FOREWORD

BY MELISSA KIM CORTER

I cherish my bond to the earth, the moon, and the land, and often felt they each had their very own unique voice and spirit. Over time, I discovered animals also had the same essence and language, speaking to us beyond words. I could feel there was so much more to their connection, yet could never describe what I felt or instinctively knew.

I met Georgia at a retreat I was co-facilitating with a few of my colleagues; she was quiet yet very kind, and I could tell she was extremely powerful at the same time. As our weekend progressed, I discovered the miraculous kinship she has with animals. They would follow her and come out of nowhere to be near her. It was no big thing for her, she would smile and shrug her shoulders. Looking back now, I see it was because that was her normal way of life.

I have always paid attention to animals, how they react to people, and if they liked someone or not. I trust in their senses above all of the capabilities of humans. We have fantastic intuition, although our minds and thoughts can get in the way; animals do not have those same obstacles, so when they bark or their hair stands up, they have my full attention.

Pet Talker: Listening to Those Who Speak Silently is a treasure. Every word helped me release my hesitations and doubts, remembering the magic in all things, especially the four legged and furry ones. I had my own remembrances of occurrences with animals and how they made me feel in their presence. Precious memories came back, ones that were buried deep within the layers of my own mind. Georgia's stories invoked my own, inviting laughter and connection into my world as I read this book. Long forgotten moments with birds in the woods, a bunny in my backyard, and the neighborhood dogs rushed in. I was overwhelmed with gratitude for this emotional awakening her book had promoted within me. I had to take some time to go outside and drink a warm cup of tea as I pondered the memories.

Suddenly, I became more aware of the birds chirping around me and hummingbirds buzzing by. It was like my ordinary world was becoming awake, alive, and filled with a fresh sense of vibrancy. Nature was speaking, always speaking, and I was now willing to hear what needed to be expressed. The trees blew with the wind, hawks danced in the sky up above, and I knew my world could never go back to being perceived through the dull and flat blanket I had thrown over it in my mind. Georgia's book had peeled back the layers, lifted a veil for me. Life was precious, and abundant, and although her book began centered around connecting with the animals, she actually became a catalyst for the messages for spirit.

I love this *book Pet Talker, Listening To Those Who Speak Silently,* and the practical tools she also provides towards the end, inviting you to establish your own way and learning the methods and possible channels for you to begin. Georgia has spent her life on this path, and is now offering you the opportunity to walk it with her, and this is such a gift. You can be just starting out and exploring your own intuitive connection, or a professional looking for a different perspective, either way, Georgia offers people of all walks of life the ability to open their mind to listen to the spirit of their animals. There is no special requirements aside from the willingness to explore and forget all you have been taught. You can do it, follow the magic and the mystery of the moment and let Georgia become your trusted companion as you learn to listen beyond words.

Georgia has taught me so much about presence, and listening to what cannot be said with words. My time with her has had a ripple effect in my own home with my two giant fur-babies. I am so blessed she has written this amazing book, opening our eyes and hearts to the language of our pets. We all have the ability to deepen our love for our animals, yet Georgia lives in the realm of this connection, making it possible and bridging the gap between us and them. She knows there is no separation, and her book is a beautiful reminder of that. I love this book and smile when I think of the stories and Georgia's innocent and playful way of showing how they are always speaking to us … we simply need to open our heart to hear them.

—**Melissa Kim Corter,** Intuitive Guide, Author & Speaker

GEORGIA NAGEL

INTRODUCTION

I am an Animal Communicator, but what does that mean? To some it might be a new fad or a new title to add to their name, to others it might be a new source of income; I am none of those. It has taken me fifty years of dedicated time with animals, and the last twenty years of working with them, seven days a week, to realize I had this ability we all have, called intuition. It was the animals that brought it to my attention, step by step, teaching me at my own pace, lessons they knew I would understand.

Today I do communicating for others, but only for the highest good of those involved and only from a place of unconditional love. It is how the animals taught me, and I respect and honor that by practicing with that intention.

This book you are holding in your hands tells of my journey from the age of three or four, my first experience with animals that I remember, to the present day. It is a compilation of the stories of the animals teaching me my communication skills, step by step, layer by layer. As the animals taught me I will be teaching you with tips, ideas, experiences, and basic tools by examples shown throughout the book.

Whether you want to learn to communicate with only your own pets or help others with their pets, this book will get you started. Remember, pets talk, we just need to learn how to listen.

GEORGIA NAGEL

CHAPTER ONE
A LIFE-CHANGING DAY

I invite you to stop ... and listen.
I encourage you to attend ... and listen.
I urge you to experience ... and listen.
~Blackwolf Jones and Gina Jones

On October 31, 2001, I went to look at a puppy a friend had told me about, the litter was free and the guy wanted to get rid of them. They were a Black Lab and Golden Retriever cross; the parents were hunting dogs. One puppy was black with a white chest and white front paws; he looked like he was wearing a tuxedo and resembled a Black Lab. The other puppy was all black except for a small white patch on his chest and resembled a black Golden Retriever. They were the only ones left and I could not take one and leave the other behind, so I drove home with two puppies, both throwing up during the forty-five-minute drive home. It was my first interaction with them, and as I would later learn, this would also become our last interaction, at the end of our journey together.

Over the years spent with these two, I would get this feeling from time to time that Midnite would not live as long as Shooz. What I did not know was these two puppies would change my life and my way of thinking forever.

The first thing I had to do was give them names, although I soon found myself calling them "boys" more often than their names. The one with the white chest and white front paws became Shooz, and the mostly black one with the wavy hair became Midnite. They had two very different personalities, with Shooz more likely to stick to the rules, only having to be told once, and Midnite more adventurous and more rebellious, kind of like me when I was younger.

Shooz would be lying on the couch or on his dog bed, while Midnite would be facing the doorway, or lying in front of the bath as I was showering. He was the protector, and anyone wanting to get to me would have to go through him first.

Four years prior to getting my dogs I had started a cleaning business and a year previous I had started a pet-sitting business. One evening after a long day of cleaning houses and making dog stops for my pet clients, I was catching up on some bookkeeping for the businesses. The boys were lying around the house napping. I logged onto my computer and began entering facts and figures. As I was doing this, Shooz came up and started nudging my right elbow with his nose, lifting it up; I assumed it was because he wanted to be petted. Shooz kept nudging my elbow and every time he did, I would hear the words "Midnite gone," another nudge, "Midnite gone."

This happened about four times before I became frustrated with trying to enter data into the computer with my right elbow bouncing all over the place. I said, "Okay, Shooz, I will pet you." I shut the computer off, turned around in my chair and started petting him.

While doing this, I looked around for Midnite, because he should have been beside me too, begging for attention. One brother could never have more attention than the other. I talked to my dogs because it was just me and them in the house. So out loud, I asked, "Shooz, where is Midnite?" I heard the word, "Gone."

In my house are two long windows about a foot from the floor facing the driveway, and one of these windows had been cranked open, with the screen missing. I walked over to the window and saw the screen lying outside on the ground and there was Midnite, coming up the driveway with a police car following him. I heard the words, "We have company."

I walked outside to talk to the police officer who was getting out of his car, and he asked if this was my dog and I said yes. I explained that he had apparently pushed the screen with his nose and jumped out the window, which was only about a three-foot drop to the ground.

The officer advised me I should do something about that window to secure it and prevent it from happening again. I assured him I would, as soon as possible.

Midnite and I went back into the house and Shooz was there to greet his brother. I got them settled and we all went to bed.

What did not register with me, but stuck in the back of my mind was that Shooz had in very simple words communicated with me, and I had not questioned it. There would be many times over the years that this would happen, but it would be awhile before I realized what was happening. Before it became natural, and I no longer questioned it.

I could be in the kitchen thinking to myself that after supper I would take the boys for a walk, and no sooner had that thought crossed my mind than they would both be in the kitchen, jumping up and down. I would say to them, "What's going on? What are you guys doing in here?"

They would just stare at me, and I would hear, "We're going for a walk."

I could be driving home on a hot summer afternoon thinking I should take the boys to the lake, and when I walked in the door they would be waiting with their lake toys at the door, ready to go.

Again, I was not registering what was going on between the three of us.

The boys worked together as a team. We would walk up the road to an open field, I would take off their leashes and they would zigzag back and forth, working the field together, looking for birds, rabbits, and whatever else they could scare up.

I could take them to the lake and if I threw the ball out too far, Midnite would go get it, because Shooz would only swim so far. Shooz weighed about 90 pounds and was much faster than Midnite, who weighed about 120 pounds.

When we played football, Shooz would go to get the football and Midnite would wait for him then tackle him and take the ball away when he got halfway back. Midnite worked and played smart, not hard, a lesson I should have learned.

When I got the pups, I put a doggy door in the side of my house along with a large outdoor kennel. The boys went through the doggy door right away; they would be chasing each other and rip the doors right out of the wall. I went through three regular-sized dog doors before I finally got one that would accommodate a Great Dane.

1 | A LIFE-CHANGING DAY

I would come home and before I got there I knew they had been up to something. What I did not know is that they were communicating with me throughout the day, I just wasn't getting it. Actually, I WAS NOT LISTENING.

One day I came home knowing I would find something in the kennel, and there was my four and half foot Ficus tree, half-in and half-out of the kennel. The two of them had somehow managed to drag it through the doggy door. I wish I would have had a hidden camera to shoot that scene. It must have been teamwork.

One afternoon I was deep cleaning, going through some papers, and as I was tossing the papers I would tear them up. I had a stack of about thirty magazines sitting on the floor. The boys had been lying on their dog beds watching me.

Seeing it was time for me to start my afternoon dog rounds, I gave each of the boys a hug and said it was time for me to go to work and that I would be home in about two hours. We had an understanding that if I told them I had to go to work, they were to stay home and not worry.

I did my dog stops, there were three, and was gone about an hour and a half. I got home, walked in the door, and found the floor was covered with about three inches of shredded magazines. While I was gone, they had shredded all thirty of those magazines. I asked, "Boys, what have you done?" I heard the words, "We helped," very clearly.

As the years went by this mode of communication continued. I would talk out loud and hear an answer. I attributed it to my imagination, like when you talk to yourself and you answer.

At the same time, the bond between me and my boys kept getting stronger. July 27, 2010, I woke up to the sound of one of the boys throwing up. I checked, and found it was Midnite.

Over the years, I had cleaned up plenty of puke piles, but I knew something was seriously wrong. The feeling I'd had all those years ago that Midnite would not live as long as Shooz proved prophetic. I took Midnite to the vet that morning and was told he had acute pancreatitis, and was very sick. I was given medications and told to boil hamburger and rice to feed him.

At home, I tried giving him the rice concoction but he refused to eat, and I could sense that he was getting sicker. Shooz and I slept on the floor next to him that night.

I took Midnite back to the vet in the morning, knowing that he would not be coming home with me. During the night, he had conveyed to me that he was very ill and it was time for me to help him go where he would no longer be in pain. The vet confirmed Midnite was not going to get any better, and it was his time to leave, whenever I was ready.

I took Midnite in my arms, kissed him, told him I loved him, and that I was so privileged to have had him in my life. I said he could let go; and within seconds he was gone. While I was sitting on the floor with him in my arms, bawling my eyes out, I felt a cool energy go through me. It had happened one other time, and I would learn later what this was.

I had Midnite cremated and it would be a week or so before I could pick up the ashes. Driving home I knew I would have to tell Shooz what happened to his brother, since they had never been separated.

In the house, I sat Shooz down beside me on Midnite's dog bed, still crying. I told him Midnite would not be with us anymore, he was very sick and he had died, it was just going to be me and him now. Shooz licked the tears from my face and got up, walked over to their dog dishes and ate Midnite's untouched food from that morning. He understood Midnite was not coming home.

1 | A LIFE-CHANGING DAY

Life went on and it had probably been about four months since Midnite had passed away, when I had a dream that was so real that I could feel Midnite's fur on my face. I did not want to wake up, but I knew he was by my side always from that moment forward.

Shooz and I kept chugging away and as the years passed our communication became even clearer. He knew my thoughts and I knew his, and working this way with him would enhance my abilities to communicate with other pets. Shooz gradually got older, moved a little slower, lost some muscle tone, started to get cataracts in his eyes and his hearing started to go. But he was my buddy and I just slowed my pace so he could keep up.

On March 17, 2016, I came home to find a puke pile on the floor, and again I knew it was serious and what I had been dreading for a long time. Shooz was lying on his dog bed, did not wag his tail, and did not want any of his jerky dog treats. I lay down on his dog bed with him; his eyes glazed over as I looked into them, and I heard the words, "Mama, it's time." Both dogs had always called me that. Shooz did not get better overnight, and the next day I called my vet and said I would be bringing him in.

We spent the morning together, he would try to follow me around like he always did, but he kept tracking to the right as if he might have suffered a stroke. I spent most of the time lying on his dog bed crying until it was time.

Ending a pet's life is never easy, but I have always been there for my animals and for my clients' pets. We were given the same room that Midnite and I had when he passed. During the day, I asked Midnite to meet his brother when Shooz crossed over, and I knew he would be waiting for him. When the veterinarian was ready to inject the shot, Shooz was lying in my lap. I said I loved him, and he was a great influence in my life, and that Midnite was waiting for him. Soon he would no longer be sick and we could still communicate. I gave him a kiss and told him to let go. Within seconds he was gone, and like before I felt a cold energy go through me.

That evening I saw an image from the two boys, they were running in an open field with tall grass just like they used to do when they were pups.

One week later I contacted a psychic medium to ask if she could see anything. I felt I knew but I was also worried that I was too close to them and my vision was only a product of my imagination. I needed another perspective. I had not told her about either one of the dogs, just that I had a business question. She answered my question and asked if I had a dog pass recently. I said I did, and she confirmed there was a dog already there, and asked which dog had the white chest. I said Shooz and he just passed away.

Then she told me the other dog had been waiting for Shooz to come to him just like I had asked. When Midnite passed, he had been very sick and she said he thanked me for helping him. He told her that when he left his body he had licked the back of my neck.

Shooz also thanked me for letting him be with me for as long as he could, but he was also very sick and needed to go. She said that their energies had passed through me, explaining the cold feeling.

She assured me they were both around me all the time and communicating with me. I thanked her for her time, and realized that she had told me everything I already knew. I just needed verification.

1 | A LIFE-CHANGING DAY

The rest of this book is about the lessons I've learned with all the animals I have worked with, and how you can also communicate with animals. Intuition is something we are all born with and we just need to exercise that muscle. I kept thinking that I needed more knowledge; that there was something I was not getting; there had to be more to this intuition thing. But I made it too complicated. The animals taught me to leave my EGO at the door if I really wanted to do this, and LISTEN. You can do this, too, so let's get started.

GEORGIA NAGEL

CHAPTER TWO
MY BEGINNING WITH ANIMALS

A nimals have been a part of my life for over fifty years. I would not have it any other way, and I am truly blessed by all my experiences with them. I was born in Iowa, my parents are George and Donna; I have a brother David, a sister Michelle, along with six nephews and two nieces, and my grandma. When I looked up the meaning of the name Georgia it said. "Of the earth, with a desire to help those around you."

My first memory of an animal was when I was between the ages of three and four. I would wake up and see an elephant standing at the end of my bed, or up against the wall. I don't remember if I cried, screamed, talked to it or did nothing at all. I still remember it after all these years, like yesterday.

When I was four we moved to a farm in Minnesota near my mom's parents and grandparents, who also lived on farms. I remember going into the farm house for the first time and the lady who lived there had cats everywhere and a sheep. I stood there with my mouth open, taking it all in. This would be my second experience with animals and I was amazed by what I was seeing. When she moved out she left most of her cats; my brother and I counted twenty-some cats outside, cats everywhere you looked.

There was one cat in particular who was not tame, and he only had one eye, the other was an empty socket. One night it was dark and I was walking out to the barn to do chores, and heard a growl. I looked around but couldn't see anything. I heard it again and I looked up, and there he was. Perched on a tree limb above the path to the barn, he was staring at me with his one good eye and the empty socket. It scared the daylights out of me, and I ran as fast as my little legs could carry me to the barn.

On our farm were dairy cows, some sheep, chickens, ducks, geese, pigs, horses, dogs and those leftover cats. Over the years we had little dogs, like Butterscotch, who was a three-legged Cocker Spaniel, and a couple of St. Bernard's, the biggest dogs we had on the farm. The St Bernard's were tough on the geese. They wanted to play, but their big paws would do damage. The geese went after them and us, pinching the skin with their bills and leaving bruises.

Our pets were in and out of the house, whatever they wanted, although some rules applied. One summer we were taking lunch out to my dad who was working in the field. Before we left my mom had taken a cake out of the oven and placed it on the table to cool so she could frost it when we got back home.

Our St. Bernard was in the house, and when we returned he was standing on the table eating the cake out of the cake pan. We kids thought it was funny, but my mom didn't find it so hilarious.

Another time we decided to take the smallest horse of the three we had, and bring him into the house. We had him halfway in the door when my mom came into the kitchen and ordered us to take him right back out the door. Have you ever tried to make a Shetland horse do something he doesn't want to do? It's not possible, since they are so stubborn.

We had chores, including milking cows, weeding the garden and field work, and we worked hard, took responsibility, and the animals on the farm depended on us for food, water, and their care.

Each of us kids were given a calf to care for, and I named mine Bo Jangles. I loved Bo Jangles and would talk to him and tell him about my day. One day Bo Jangles would not eat, he was sick and then he died. I cried and cried. I could not figure out at my young age why loving something so much could not make it better. One of life's painful truths learned early on.

The Dog Years

After graduating from high school, I found myself collecting dogs; there must have been a "softie" sticker on my forehead. The start of the collection were two lab-mix puppies (is there a pattern here?) I found at a flea market. They were free and I could not take one and leave the other. Driving home, I remembered my brother's anniversary was coming up, so he and his wife's gift were the two puppies.

The next was a husky-wolf cross the owners could not use for sled-dog racing because she was too timid. Her name was Joy and she was also free. I brought her out to my parents' house to join a little Chihuahua I had rescued named TC.

My sister and I rented a house together, and one night I went to the grocery store. A little boy was standing outside the store entrance holding a puppy in his arms. It was fall, raining and cold, he was shivering and so was the puppy. He was crying and begging people to take his puppy or his dad was going to shoot the dog. I came home with groceries and a puppy we named Boots.

After that, a Samoyed wandered onto a turkey farm and needed rescuing. I drove out to get him and named him Sam, not too creative, I know. Sam was a unique dog. In the spring, he would stand in the lake and as the sucker fish would swim between his legs, he would bark and bark and put his head under the water and come up with a fish in his mouth.

Sam also had a bad habit of barking at skunks. He thought they were black-and-white cats until one sprayed him between the eyes. He would grab them, give them one shake and break their necks. When he got sprayed he smelled like skunk. I asked mom and grandma how to get rid of the smell and was told tomato juice. I took some home-canned tomato juice and poured it all over him. My white dog was pink for two months.

Later I would buy another Samoyed, the first dog I paid for. Sam Zak Kodiak's nemesis was garter snakes. Sam Zak would live a long life.

I then took a break from dogs until I got my two boys, Shooz and Midnite.

Odd Occurrences

During the early dog years things happened that I thought were normal but others might think differently. The first I can remember was when I was about the age of sixteen or seventeen. I had what I called a dream (somebody told me later they could be called visions) of two boys in the area we all knew who had been in a car accident. They had rolled a car, but they were both okay. I told my mom the next morning. I don't think she thought much of it until later that day when we heard the news confirming it.

I also dreamed that Roy Orbison died, and told my mom. This time she gave me a strange look then went back to what she was doing. His death was announced that day.

In my early thirties, I noticed a phenomenon that started the week of O.J. Simpson's white bronco chase, June 1994. All that week I was in despair and could not stop crying. I had never felt like this, and thought I should go see my ex-husband. The feeling was that someone would die, and I was sure it was me.

The Friday night they were chasing OJ in that Bronco, I got a call from a friend who said my ex-husband had crashed his van and was dead. We had been divorced for seven years, but his roommate and I were the ones who planned his funeral. The visitation was in the afternoon and it was unusually warm for June, almost ninety degrees that day. The air conditioning was not working in the chapel. As I was halfway up the aisle walking to the casket I felt a gust of cold air pass right through me. I would not think of that again until Shooz passed and then I remembered the same thing happened with Midnite. It was their energy going through me, or some would say their soul.

The despair was to continue. The next time it happened my friend's daughter died, and then a couple more friends passed away and it was always the same, so much crying. I finally asked myself, what good is this doing me? I can't do anything about it and I don't want to feel it anymore. It stopped shortly after that.

In my late thirties, I went to see a gentleman who read rune stones, which are rocks painted with symbols. This was all new to me but a friend had recommended him. At his shop, I sat down at the table, and he asked me to hold out my hands, palms up, and cup them together. He poured the stones into my palms and then he put his hands above mine, without touching them. I soon felt the stones starting to move in my palms. He asked if I felt that, and I said, "You mean the stones shifting?"

He replied, "Yes." He then told me he had been reading stones for many years but they had never done that.

He then did an experiment. He lit a candle and then asked me to think of something or someone that made me very angry. This was not too difficult, because that was why I was there. I wanted to know about a bad relationship and if I should leave it.

So, I thought about this person and soon I heard the candle sputtering like it was going out. He then asked me to think of something that made me happy.

He told me that when I was angry the candle almost went out, and when happy the flame shot right back up.

My explanation for that now is everything is energy and energy was reacting to energy. I thought this happened to everyone.

In my forties, I took an afternoon intuition class, since strange events were happening with animals and I wanted an explanation. I was convinced that this could not be as simple as it seemed; it had to be more complex. About eight were in the class, and after a brief introduction we got down to business. We partnered with the person to the right of us, one of us to be the receiver and the other the sender.

My partner and I decided I was to be the receiver. The sender was to think of something yellow, and I was to try to receive it. I soon was getting a yellow caution sign, the sun, and a bowl of lemons and a pitcher of lemonade. We went around the room and the receivers told what they saw and the senders what they sent. One had thought of the sun, one a bowl of lemons, and one a pitcher of lemonade. I thought, "I received all of those images."

The teacher then asked my partner what she had sent me and her reply was, "I first considered the sun but that was too simple, then I thought about a caution sign, but I wanted something more difficult. So, I thought of that toy cone with rings from large to small in different colors."

My heart sank. I was no good at this, I could not pick up on what she had been thinking. The teacher asked me what I had received, and I said at first I got a caution sign, then the sun, and then a bowl of lemons, and a pitcher of lemonade but no baby toy. The instructor said, "Your partner could not make up her mind and was not sending anything clear. You moved on to what others were sending, which were clearer pictures."

Lesson: If things are not clear, you might receive information from a stronger signal. That is why you might go to a medium or a psychic to hear from a person that has passed, but be given a message from someone else. They may have a stronger signal the psychic picks up.

The same goes with animals, you may be around more than one animal, and receive a few messages all at once from all of them, but one may be clearer than the others.

It was now my turn to think of something for my partner to receive. The instructor said the color was green, and right away I thought of a field with tall green grass blowing in the breeze, with the sun shining and trees along the edge of the field. My partner got everything I pictured, and the instructor said it was because I had been very clear about what I was visualizing and transmitting.

Next, we partnered with the person to the left of us. We had all been asked to bring a picture of our pet to class. We swapped pictures and wrote down our thoughts on their pet. Kelly got that Shooz was a proud dog, smart, and something about a radio and that he was ok with that music channel. Kelly was correct; I had just started leaving the radio on for him when I left for work, since he was alone. And I had been wondering if he liked the station.

It was my turn to pick up information on her dog, Gus. I looked at his picture and could see him in my mind chasing squirrels. I knew somehow that Gus had a fun personality and wanted a Buddy. So, I told her the first two things and she verified them. I then told her Gus wanted a Buddy, a friend, someone to play with. Kelly said the dog next-door was named Buddy and they played together often.

I left class that day with a little more understanding of what I was experiencing and thought maybe it was not as complicated as my ego made it out to be. I would learn more about what a hindrance my ego could be later on.

The above are examples of exercises you can do with a friend or family member to start using that muscle called intuition. You might find yourself thinking, "Is it just my imagination or was that a lucky guess?" or maybe, "I knew that and just didn't remember it." This is your ego trying to protect you and keep you in a safe zone. If you can, try to put your ego aside; we will learn more about this in the chapter on tools. A quick note about your ego: it likes to keep the status quo, and it does not like change.

CHAPTER THREE
LISTEN TO THE BIG DOGS

Russell

The second time I realized that a dog was communicating with me was with a Great Pyrenees named Russell. I still did not know what this was called or exactly what was happening. Russell's pet parents, Jon and Michelle (Mitch), had contacted me about pet-sitting for Russell a couple times a week in the afternoons. I went over to their house to meet Russell, who was very protective of them and the house. I spent time talking to Russell and petting him and he eventually accepted my presence there and let me know that we would get along fine.

It was probably a couple months into my coming over to the house and taking Russell for his afternoon walks that Jon and Michelle decided to take advantage of my other business. They asked if I would be interested in cleaning their house. I found a spot where I could work them into my schedule and started cleaning for them.

The days I was there to clean their house, Russell would be out in his kennel, and he never seemed happy about me going into the house since he was so protective. I could see it in his eyes. One afternoon I was taking Russell for his walk, and I had a picture in my mind of Russell with my left forearm in his mouth. Two seconds later Russell had my left forearm in his mouth, and I did not yank my arm away. I just said to Russell, "No, let go of my arm," and he released his hold. I knew it was a warning because he barely broke the skin and he could have done damage if he had so desired. But I did not understand the warning.

Jon and Michelle decided maybe the walks should end, but the house cleaning could continue. I started to watch Russell when I would come to clean their house, and he was fine with me until I would go into the house and then he would get crabby. I decided to conduct an experiment. While I was out taking care of another pet in their area, I stopped to see Russell but did not enter his house. He was absolutely fine with that. I had my answer to why he had given me a warning. I was not to go into his house; it was his domain, his space.

The fact that I had seen him grab my arm a split-second before it happened had me puzzled, and then I remembered Shooz talking to me when I heard the words, "Midnite gone." What was happening to me? I did some research and found this was called animal communication, but I couldn't believe it was something I could do. Again, I was wrong. It was occurring so often that I could not ignore it.

Being shown a picture in my mind of Russell with my forearm in his mouth before it happened is called clairvoyance, and means "clear vision." When I heard Shooz tell me, "Midnite gone," was clairaudience, and means "clear hearing." We will discuss both abilities and many more in **Chapter Twelve: Tools.**

Knuckles

Knuckles was a Greyhound whose pet parents were Jerry and Sherri. They had two other dogs in their house, a Black Lab named Stout and a Boxer named Kadi. All were three older dogs. The dogs were pet-sitting clients of mine on a regular basis. Each one had a different personality and I enjoyed taking care of them. Jerry and Sherri decided to take a cruise one winter, with their daughter staying at the house for the weekend, and I would start late Sunday night.

Sunday morning I got a frantic call from their daughter saying something was wrong with Knuckles, she thought he might have had a grand mal seizure. I called their veterinarian on the way out to their house, he also agreed it was probably a seizure and not much could be done, but to keep him updated.

When I got to their house, Knuckles did not look good, he was lying down and very weak. The daughter had talked to Jerry and Sherri and they asked us to try to keep Knuckles alive till they returned from their cruise, which was a week. I lay down on the floor next to Knuckles and petted him and talked to him. He would not eat or drink, but with help he could go outside to do his business. Something told me that food was not important right now but I had to keep him hydrated. I could get a turkey baster and fill it with an electrolytes drink, open Knuckles mouth and squirt it into his throat.

I headed into town for my supplies, checking with the veterinarian, and he said all that would work. The next two days and nights I spent lying on the floor with Knuckles when I was not making my pet-sitting stops. I would get fluids in him until he would not let me, then I would stand him up, put a bath towel underneath his belly and support him down the three steps and out into the yard so he could do his duty. I'd then put the towel back under his belly and up the stairs we would go, into the house.

During this time, I had this "knowing" that it was not his time yet and he just needed a lot of love and patience to get through this. I think it was Thursday when he started to get better. He would get up and move around, drink water out of his dish, but would not eat.

While in town I decided to pick up plain hamburgers at McDonalds and see if he would eat them. I only picked up two, and he scarfed them down, no problem. Next time I went into town I got more burgers, and he was loving life. Jerry and Sherri got home that Saturday and Knuckles was now moving around, eating, drinking, just like when they left, although it took a while to wean him off the burgers, since he now preferred them over dry food.

Knuckles would live a couple more years after that episode; he had another seizure while they were gone, but pulled through that one too. When it was his end of life I went into the veterinarians with Jerry.

This adventure with Knuckles gave me an awareness of another ability I would learn about, claircognizance, meaning "clear knowing." We will discuss more about this later in the book.

Mi'Lady

Mi'Lady is an English springer spaniel who was rescued by Jodi. I learned about Mi'Lady while I was trying to figure out Facebook. I had opened a Facebook account for my business but did not spend much time reading the posts. Things happen for a reason, I believe, and one day I was drawn to read a post by Jodi. She was asking anyone for ideas; she had taken Mi'Lady to several vets and they could not figure out why she was itching nonstop. Jodi had tried various remedies but nothing was working. I thought to myself when I read her post, this is an emotional issue, not physical.

A couple days later I was reading on Facebook again, and Jodi was still looking for some help with Mi'Lady. I messaged her with my phone number and asked her to call me about Mi'Lady. Jodi called and I told her that I thought this was an emotional problem with Mi'Lady and Jodi shared that she had rescued the dog.

I asked Jodi if she would mind if I tried to communicate with Mi'Lady, that sometimes I could get information, and she said to go ahead. I was able to determine the underlying causes, which Jodi validated, along with other information that surprised both of us, especially me.

I offered to bring essential oils to help Mi'Lady recover, and Jodi agreed. We found which oils were the most beneficial to Mi'Lady. Jodi continued to use the oils and eventually the problems that had been troubling Mi'Lady left her. Mi'Lady is now a happy dog with no itching, and Jodi and she are enjoying life together. This story is an example of Claircognizance, Clairvoyance and Clairaudience.

Yeti

Yeti is a Border collie mix whose pet mom is Rose. I have been taking care of Yeti as a pet-sitting client during the noon hour, five days a week for over three years. Yeti is a very intelligent dog, with a fun, sarcastic personality. Yeti and I communicate much like I did with my boys Shooz and Midnite. I say something and she responds; we can carry on a conversation of short sentences. I have found that most things animals say are short, sweet, and to the point.

Yeti has over seventy-five toys and they all have names. If you piled Yeti's toys together and named one, she would dig through the heap and bring it to you, which she does with Rose all the time. The problem is I do not know the correct name for all the toys so I will say what I think the toy should be called and she will tilt her head and stare at me quizzically.

I'll hear Yeti ask, "Try again," and at this point I'll usually just picture the toy in my mind and she'll get it.

One day we were playing with her Frisbee, and I decided to try a fancy trick. I threw it to her, she let it land at her feet and I could sense she was disgusted. I said, "What?"

Yeti asked, "What was that?"

I replied, "A trick."

Yeti answered, "I do the tricks here," and she picked up the Frisbee and brought it to me to throw again.

I could not help but chuckle; I was now being scolded by a dog. I have learned from spending so much time with Yeti that she is quite the perfectionist and believes she is the leader of her pack.

Yeti goes everywhere with Rose, paddle-boarding with Yeti on the board, diving off of Rose's pontoon into the lake, and she enjoys kayaking, camping, and biking. She is a well-behaved, smart dog, and I have learned much from her.

Shooz

In the fall, I try to get away for a few days when things slow down in my pet-sitting business. The last couple of years I took Shooz to stay with my friends Nancy and Lowell while I was gone. He loved his time with them, and we called it Camp Nereson. I would buy him a new dog bed, bags and bags of treats, dry dog food, wet dog food, new toys (you would think I was going for a month), and then load this all up along with some old toys, a dog leash, his dog dishes, and Shooz. I'd take him there the night before I left and get him settled in.

Nancy and I put most of his stuff in the dining room where Shooz could see her in the kitchen, since his hearing was pretty much gone. I would kiss him goodbye, tell him I would be back in four days at bright time, which means daylight, and to be a good boy.

The second day into his stay, Shooz was lying on his dog bed, Nancy was in the kitchen and Lowell was in the living room watching the news on the television. Nancy asked Lowell if he was hungry and would he like something to eat for supper. Lowell said yes, he was getting hungry.

Shooz got up from his dog bed and went to his pile of treats, picked up an unopened bag with his teeth, and brought it into the living room and dropped it at Lowell's feet. Lowell still chuckles about that day. They could not believe it, but Shooz had been with me all those years and had become so accustomed to tuning into my thoughts and words that he picked up on their discussion, and responded to it.

That was another validation for me of the special bond I shared with Shooz. It was too bad Midnite couldn't put in his two cents' worth. I would learn later that he was helping me all along.

Ginger

Ginger was an older chocolate Lab when I first started pet-sitting for her owners, GL and Deb. I remember Ginger well; she would look at you out of the corner of her eye and tilt her head. When we took walks, she had her own pace, and we could only go back to the house when she was ready, not before.

As Ginger aged her hearing started to go, and I would come into the house and she wouldn't notice. I never want to startle a dog, especially an older dog, since I know it's a matter of pride for them. They are supposed to be keeping an eye on the house, and it would mean somebody had entered the house and they didn't know it.

When this would happen, I would offhandedly talk to her and sometimes place my hand in front of her nose so she could smell me and slowly wake up.

I was taking care of Ginger about the time things were happening with other dogs like Russell and Shooz. One day I came into the house and she had not heard me, so I decided to play scientist.

Ginger was lying on her chair, sound asleep and not moving, perfectly content. I wanted to test my animal communication skills, so I sat in a chair across the room from her. She couldn't see me or smell me, and she was facing away from me. In my mind I said silently, "Ginger, wake up. Ginger, should we go for a walk?"

I did this a couple times and she didn't respond, so I woke her up gently by talking softly to her and letting her smell my hand. Ginger woke up and we went for our walk.

The next day I repeated the process all over again, and again nothing happened. It was on my third visit that I figured I'd try one more time and if I was not able to do what I thought I could, I would give up. (This was my ego talking. My ego did not want me to do this because it was comfortable where I was in my life. If there was a change, what would people think?)

I sat across the room from Ginger again, and began talking silently in my head to her. "Ginger, do you want to go outside? Ginger, do you want to go for a walk? Ginger, wake up, let's go for a walk."

And then it happened. I saw her paws start to move back and forth, one in front of the other. I again said silently, "Let's walk, Ginger."

Her tail started to thump the chair she was lying on, her eyes began to flutter. Ginger had heard me telepathically. I was so happy, and then my ego stepped in and started to use reason, telling me it was just coincidence, I did not communicate with her, she was dreaming, and when dogs dream, they sometimes move their feet.

So, I decided on my next visit I would try it again. I went through the whole process and the same thing happened. Ginger heard me, confirming we were on the same wavelength, the same frequency.

One day I got a call from her owner Deb to say they had put Ginger down. I wept just as I do when I hear that any of my pet clients have reached the end of their lives. I still miss Ginger. She had such a sweet demeanor, and when I visit her house to walk their new dog, Gracie, I ask Ginger if she wants to come along with us. Deb takes Gracie to volunteer with the local Hospice in our town. Gracie dons her little vest and knows the word work. She takes her job seriously.

GEORGIA NAGEL

CHAPTER FOUR
LITTLE DOGS, BIG VOICES

Charlie and Sophie

In the early years of pet-sitting, I was taking care of a pair of Basset Hounds, Charlie and Sophie. They lived with their pet parents Brad and Barb, on the edge of town. This would be my third experience with animal communication and I still did not know what it was all about, just that I was hearing voices in my head and the animals were responding.

Charlie and Sophie were great dogs but typical Bassets; they had their own pace and those "booming" voices that Bassets are known for when they bark. I had been taking care of these two for four or five years when the sleeping arrangements changed. The dogs were older and would be put in designated areas at night. With this new placement came the issue of each being in a separate crate.

I came over one evening to feed them and let them out to roam their fenced-in backyard before returning to their crates for the evening. Everything was going great just as it always had;

these two were not difficult dogs. The crates were side by side, and I told the dogs to "kennel up" and then they would get their treats.

Charlie went into his kennel so I gave him his treat and shut the crate door. I turned to Sophie who was standing by the door, and said, "Sophie, kennel up," but she ran into another room. These two had always shared a space and they listened and minded well. What was going on?

I tried again, "Sophie, kennel up," and she wouldn't budge. As I have said before, I am always talking out loud to the animals as if I were having a conversation with a person. So out loud, I asked, "Sophie, what is wrong, why won't you go into your crate?"

I was surprised when I heard back, "Charlie mean."

I thought to myself, what did I just hear? I tried to put Sophie in her crate again, she would not move, and I tried again. "Sophie what's wrong?"

I heard back again, "Charlie mean," so I decided to see if this was true about Charlie.

I put Sophie in her crate and shut the door. Immediately Charlie tried to attack her through the crates. I let Sophie out of her crate and moved it from the hallway into the living room where they could both see each other but not be next to each other. I told Sophie to "kennel up" and she went right into her crate. I gave them both their treats for the night.

This is another example of Clairaudience (clear hearing), and in the beginning this ability was more pronounced for me, and how I most-often received messages. Sophie lived a longer life than Charlie, and moved into a new home with Barb and Brad, where I still would pet-sit for her. During those times, Barb and I would discuss Sophie's aging and failing abilities. They knew, as do all pet owners, that a day will come when we must say goodbye, and I finally received that call from Barb, which is never easy.

More Bassets

Beth and Paul are big-time Basset Hound lovers; they have adopted seven Basset Hounds: Kirby, Howard, Bailey, Buster, Boomer, Flash and Sophie. They have also fostered three Basset Hounds, Chocolate, Fred and a female. Once they adopt a Basset it will stay in their family until it passes.

I started pet-sitting for them first, then as others have done they wished to use my cleaning service. I did not get to spend much time with Howard and Kirby, one of the two had already gone on and the other followed shortly afterward. Bailey was a cranky older Basset, and as soon as I met her I called her Miss Bailey. She had a personality that demanded respect as she tottered around their home.

Paul had put in a doggy door and Beth and I were trying to teach Bailey how to go in and out. One of us would stand outside the house and the other inside. We held the door open and tried to coax Bailey out with a hamburger, treats, all kinds of goodies, but she would not go through the dog door. I told Beth, she knows how to use this dog door, she is not a dumb dog.

Three or four days after our venture to get Bailey through the dog door, I was at their house cleaning, working in the kitchen when I heard the dog door swing shut. I looked out the kitchen window, which overlooked the fenced yard and the dog door, and there was Bailey standing outside on the steps.

Paul was home and I said to him, "Did you hear that? Bailey

just went through the dog door!" We heard the dog door again; Bailey had just come back into the house through the doggy door. I knew all along that she could use it and was just being stubborn, but I didn't know how I knew.

Buster was living at another home I was cleaning on a regular basis, and when that family said they had to find a home for him, I immediately thought of Paul and Beth. I told Beth about it, she contacted the family and Buster came to live with them.

I remember the first day I came to clean at Beth and Paul's house right after Buster moved in. I entered their house and Buster was so excited to see me, and then I heard the words, "Where you been?" from Buster.

I chuckled to myself while I thought, "You are so vain, Buster, of course it is all about you."

He was such a loving dog and had a great personality. I would often meet Beth on the road and Buster would be hanging out the window with his ears blowing in the wind. Buster also loved to hang in the wind on their boats.

Boomer was named appropriately, he had a massive, booming voice, and was an older dog when Beth and Paul adopted him, but he fit in well with Buster and Bailey. Beth would venture to Basset Fest in Wisconsin with the three dogs and Boomer won an award or two. As Boomer got even older, Beth had me come over and do Reiki on Boomer for his joints. I would sit on the floor and ask Boomer where he would like to receive his Reiki treatment. He would position his body into my hands where he needed the extra energy. Boomer would then get up and take a big drink of water and I would know he'd had enough for the day.

Flash was an awesome dog, and he loved to talk. I once

picked him up from a grooming appointment because Beth was delayed in a meeting, and he talked all the way home, which I recorded for Beth. I will be talking about Flash in a later chapter.

Sophie is a petite, little Basset, and the sweetheart of the group. The first time I met her she was a little timid initially, but warmed up fast, thanks to her home environment. Sophie and I developed an understanding after the first visit, when I took care of her and the other dogs.

Sophie would not eat her food, and I didn't think too much of it because some dogs won't eat when their owners are gone. I came back that evening and she still would not eat, so I went to the fridge. Beth sometimes gives them people food and I wondered what I could find.

I came up with parmesan cheese in a shaker container and shook it over her food while I said, "Do you want some sprinkles?" and then did the same to the other dog dishes.

It was probably a month or so before I came back to watch the dogs for Beth and Paul, and when Sophie would not eat, I said, "Sophie, eat."

She just looked at me, so I said, "Sophie, why won't you eat?"

I heard my answer, "Sprinkles."

It took me a minute before I remembered what sprinkles were. I went to the fridge and found the cylinder with parmesan cheese, shook some cheese on her food and she ate. Of course, the other dogs now wait for the sprinkles on their food and this has become a ritual when I am there.

Chocolate was a foster dog staying at Beth and Paul's for a week while on his way to his new home. I was lucky enough to be at their home cleaning so I could experience what a wonderful dog he was.

I was not having a good day before I arrived at their house, but that changed when the dogs greeted me at the door. I spent some time with them and the new little boy Chocolate. I started cleaning but my mood was sad. Apparently, Chocolate picked up on my emotion, because he came bounding down the hall with a flower bigger than he was, clamped in his mouth and presented it to me.

His gesture brought tears to my eyes, it still does. I had just met him that day and he picked up on my sadness and did something about it. I had to call Beth and tell her. She was not sure where he had found the flower, but was also moved by his act of kindness.

Because I have talked so much about Paul and Beth's Bassets, I must mention the other dog in the family, the first non-Basset. She was rescued by Paul when he was on the road for work. Brinn is a Pit Bull mix, and was in rough shape when Paul found her. She is now in great shape and fits in well with the family, a happy dog.

Here is a little test to see if you recognize some of the "Clairs" I have been talking about in the above Basset Stories. Write down your answer to each one listed.

Bailey's Story: _____

Buster's Story: _____

Boomer's Story: _____

Sophie's Story: _____

The answers are: Bailey and Boomer's stories are about Claircognizance {Clear Knowing}, and Buster and Sophie's stories are about Clairaudience {Clear Hearing}

CHAPTER FIVE
I JUST KNOW

Maizey

Maizey was a little Shih Tzu, but her pet parents Greg and Gina sometimes called her breed "Pure Sassy" because of her personality. I started pet-sitting for Maizey when she was about six or seven years old and they were living out in the country. Greg and Gina then moved into town and I was not needed as often. Maizey was a bit older when I stated sitting for them again.

Gina called one day and asked if I was available to watch Maizey for the weekend. I agreed and we set up the schedule. She said they were worried about Maizey because she was not eating, her appetite was gone.

My first stop to see her was in the evening. I let Maizey out, we walked around the yard and then we came back into the house for her supper. Now I have to tell you, Maizey was spoiled. She had paper plates in the fridge with several meats and a variety of cheeses, and they looked good enough to be served at a cocktail party. I set a prepared plate on the floor. Maizey took one look at it and walked away. I wasn't concerned since she had dry food, and I am most concerned that they drink water, and are not throwing up or have diarrhea.

When I came back later for bedtime, I took her outside, we went for a walk and when we came back in I tried to coax her into eating the food again, with no luck. So, I left it for her to munch on during the night in case she decided to eat.

The next morning, I took her outside and we walked around then came back into the house for breakfast. I threw away the plate she did not touch from the night before, and got a new one out of the fridge and placed it on the floor. I sat down beside the plate and tried to hand-feed the meat and cheeses to her. With no interest from Maizey, I pretended to eat some of the food, but still had no reaction from Maizey. She just looked at me.

I said out loud, "Maizey, why won't you eat this good food?"

To my surprise I heard a response, "Maizey eats on china."

I thought, "What?" Then it came to me. Maizey did not like the paper plates, so I took a glass plate from the cupboard, transferred the food, and she ate it.

In Maizey's neighborhood, a little white dog lives on the corner and he can see Maizey's house from his window. He watches and waits for Maizey to go outside then he rushes over. The little white dog's name is Charlie and he loves Maizey, but the feeling is not mutual.

Maizey and I were outside when Charlie came running up to greet us, his tail wagging, such a happy boy. I bent down and petted him. He then went over to greet Maizey. She snapped and growled at him, and walked back toward the house to go inside. As I let her in the house I said out loud to Maizey, "Can you tell me what that was about?"

Maizey replied, "He is beneath me." I realized that Maizey was a "little diva," and considered herself a princess.

When Gina and Greg got back I told Gina to buy a china plate for Maizey and see if that made a difference in her appetite, because she did not think she should be eating on paper plates.

I also informed her that Maizey had no time for Charlie, but she did like the two big dogs that lived right next door, Apollo and Bode, with their pet parents Michael and Betsy.

Gina informed me that Maizey would sit on the bathroom counter in the mornings while Gina got ready for work, and Maizey would stare at herself in the mirror.

Gina and Greg did buy Maizey a fancy plate and her appetite returned. They did a little test and put Maizey's favorite food, hamburger, on a paper plate and she refused to eat it; they then put it on her fancy plate and she ate it. Gina and Greg were happy because she had been getting so thin from not eating.

Maizey the little "Princess Diva" would live another two or three years before she passed away at thirteen-and-a-half years old. I miss her and her strong personality.

This story is another example of Clairaudience (clear hearing). When I talk about the animals replying or I say I hear them, I am hearing or receiving verbal messages in my head, and the pets are not talking out loud to me. They all have different personalities, so some are louder than others, just like humans.

In Maizey's story, claircognizance (clear knowing) was when I knew she had an aversion to the paper plates. Many times you will experience different Clairs at the same time when you tune into your intuition.

P.J.

P.J. was a Pomeranian and along with a cat named Melissa, lived with their pet parents, Walt and Pat, an older couple. P.J. lived in the south during the winter and came to Minnesota in the summertime. Walt and the cat Melissa would drive and Pat and P.J. would fly, with P.J. in a pet carrier on the plane.

Pat and Walt were among the very first pet-sitting clients I had and I loved visiting with them when they would come back to Minnesota in the spring. Pat's stipulation in pet-sitting was that I stay overnight with P.J. and Melissa and at that time because I did not have many clients, I could do that. The reason for staying was that P.J. was fearful during thunderstorms; she would become so excited that she had to take a pill so she could breathe. I was to stay at their cabin on the lake and it was to be a mini-vacation for me, too.

Pat and Walt were going to a class reunion one weekend in June and wanted me to stay with P.J. and Melissa. At their cabin, I was given instructions and told if it stormed I was to give P.J. her pill.

The first night I was there it did not storm; the second night there was a thunderstorm. P.J., Melissa and I had gone to bed, with P.J. asleep on the bed with me; and Melissa on her favorite spot, the bunk-beds in the other bedroom.

It was about one in the morning when I heard the wind start to pick up. This cabin had been in the family for many generations, an older cabin with little insulation so it was not soundproof. As the wind grew stronger I could see off in the distance lightning flash against the dark sky, but no thunder.

I looked at P.J., sound sleep at my feet, and thought it must be the thunder that bothered her, so no pill yet.

About fifteen minutes later, I could hear the rain pounding on the roof and beating against the windows. The lightning was now lighting up the sky and the wind was howling. Then came a loud crack of thunder, sounding like it hit close to the cabin.

To let you know, I am not afraid of storms. I respect them but do not get agitated. I have been in storms with trees falling down around me and the wind sounding like a train barreling through the backyard.

With this loud crack of thunder, I expected P.J. to wake up and start shaking. Nope, she was sound asleep. I woke her up and told her it was storming out, and she just looked at me and went back to sleep.

Within twenty minutes the storm had passed and left only a gentle rain. I did not give P.J. her pill that night, she did not need it, but I did lay awake wondering why she did not freak out like Pat said she would. Why didn't I have a frightened, nervous, scared dog? Then it came to me. P.J. was not reacting to the storms; she was mirroring Pat's reaction to storms.

A few days after they were home from the reunion I stopped by to visit. I asked Pat how she felt about storms and she said they frightened her. She had lived in a hurricane area years earlier and every time it stormed she relived her fears.

I then told Pat about P.J.'s experience with the thunder when she was with me, and my observation that it was not the storms that had P.J. worked up, it was Pat's terror. That marked the end of P.J.'s need for medication during thunderstorms. P.J., Melissa, Walt and Pat have all passed on, and I miss them all very much. They were a wonderful family.

Meg

Meg was rescued by her pet parents Elliot and Katee, and lives with them and a cat named Rose in the country. I was contacted by Katee and Elliot to ask if I could pet-sit while they attended a wedding out of town. I could and we agreed on an initial visit

I do a meet-and-greet with every customer. This way, the pets are familiar with me when their parents leave. I think this makes the experience easier on the animals.

The evening I came to Elliot and Katee's home I walked in the front door but was not greeted by pets, just Elliot. We went into the kitchen and I chatted with Elliot, who detailed Meg's behavior. I began to think Elliot was not sure how Meg would react to me, but he was quick to assure me she had never bitten anyone. Meg barked but she was a timid dog, he said.

Elliot said if Meg would not let me into the house that was ok, not to worry, just text or call them.

I finally said to Elliot, "Let's just let her out of the garage and see how she does. We'll be fine." I knew somehow that it was not Meg that was getting all worked up, it was Elliot, and she was picking up on his energy when meeting new people. I suggested to Elliot that he not be so apprehensive about Meg.

Elliot let Meg into the house. I started talking to her, and she smelled my hand with her tail wagging. I gave her a treat and we were friends. There were none of the issues that Elliot was concerned about that weekend. Meg, Rose and I got along perfectly. She is a great dog and well behaved, she listens, she did not rip anything up, and she ate her food.

I called Elliot the next week and told him I had no issues with Meg, and that the fears he had expressed were about what he was expecting would happen. Elliot told me the first night they were gone that they both kept checking their phones for a call or text from me that Meg would not let me in the house. They eventually quit checking and enjoyed their weekend away.

While we were visiting the night of the meet-and-greet, we also talked about various foods for Meg as she was having some eating problems. I offered some ideas to correct that, and Elliot later told me they took my advice and Meg's fur was much better, along with her digestion. I loved spending time with Meg and looked forward to seeing her again.

Animals are very receptive to our energy and our emotions; they pick up on our feelings easily. That is why sometimes you see an animal with the same hyper energy of its owner. Whether you believe it or not, they can discern what you are thinking, and if you keep thinking your pet is going to jump on people or that it is going to run away, or even bite someone, it just might, because it feels the energy you are putting out into the universe. That is also why you can be very sad and they will come over to comfort you by licking your face. They feel that you are sad.

Dogs and horses can sense fear in a person, and they will react to that by scaring you or actually biting you. They will feed off that emotion of fear you send out.

Rosie

Rosie is an enthusiastic Black Lab, to say the least; she is full of energy, but a sweet dog. Rosie has another dog in her family named Jackson, a Bernese mountain dog, and their pet parents are Mark and Cindy.

When I come to their house for pet sitting, I will open the door and out goes Rosie, looking for a ball or hockey puck. Jackson saunters out and waits until I'm not looking then will come up behind me and run between my legs. Jackson is a big dog and it took me by surprise the first time it happened, as I almost fell over. But he stops between my legs and expects me to pet him and hug him. He wants me to scratch his back and massage his legs; he has this all figured out.

Rosie in the meantime has a ball in her mouth, waiting for me to throw it so she can play fetch.

Cindy contacted me to ask if I could watch the dogs over a weekend and I told her I could. That Saturday afternoon, I walked into the house and knew instantly something was very wrong. Jackson was hyper and Rosie was just shaking and wouldn't move. For a second I wondered what it was, then I immediately knew: it was the underground fence collar Rosie wore around her neck. It must have been shocking her.

I took the collar off Rosie, brought it to a different room, and came back to her and Jackson. She was still shaking, so I grabbed a bath towel and wrapped it around her shoulders and back. I then sat on the floor and pulled Rosie onto my lap and just held her while I talked to her. She eventually calmed down. I put a leash on her and Jackson, and we went outside to walk. I knew if I could get Rosie relaxed Jackson would also relax.

When it came time to go back in the house Rosie was a little hesitant, but I told her it would be all right, and of course treats helped. I explained to Cindy what I thought was happening with the underground fence collar, that it was shorting out and giving Rosie shocks in the house and I had removed her collar.

When Mark and Cindy got home they had the underground fence checked and learned there was a break in the wire and it was giving off random mini shocks. The fence is now fixed and the household is back to normal.

How did I know there was a short in the fence collar, how did I know that Elliot was the issue with Meg, or that Pat was the issue with P.J.? It is called Claircognizance, clear knowing, and when the knowledge comes to me, I ask myself later, "How did I know that?" I know it, but I don't know how I know it. We will go into this more in a later chapter.

GEORGIA NAGEL

CHAPTER SIX
THE CAT'S MEOW

As I started this chapter, I thought of a movie I had seen on television when I was young. A Walt Disney movie, it was about a cat named Thomasina and a little girl whose dad was a veterinarian. His wife had died and he was a bitter man. A woman lived in the village who the young kids called a witch because she had a way with animals. Thomasina gets hurt, the girl takes the cat to her dad the vet, and he puts the cat down, or so he thought. The kids hold a funeral for the cat, the woman sees the funeral and when the children leave she takes the cat home with her and nurses it back to health.

Somehow the little girl sees the cat and follows it in a rainstorm, but cannot keep up with it. The little girl gets very ill, and the cat's memory returns. It sits at the little girl's window, but won't go in because it sees the child's dad by her bedside.

Eventually Thomasina changes her mind and the cat is reunited with the little girl and all is well.

I did not realize until now what an impact that story had on me, along with "Old Yeller," a Disney movie about a dog, and the "Wizard of Oz," which upset me when the flying monkeys took Toto the dog.

These movies resonated with me. They ignited my fierce love for animals and all creatures of this earth.

Maharshi

Maharshi was the first cat I heard, or I should say, the first I heard and understood clearly. Rishi (the shortened version of his name) was one of the few cats I cared for in my early years of pet sitting.

Jeanne, Rishi's pet parent, called and asked if I could watch Rishi for a few days while she was away. We set up a time for me to meet both of them.

I arrived at their home and was greeted by Jeanne, a wonderful woman who made me feel right at home. I loved her energy. We discussed the feeding instructions and litter box detail. I then asked to meet Rishi, because thus far I had not seen or heard him. We went into the living room and I sat on the couch and Jeanne took a chair to my right.

While we were talking, Rishi came into the room and sat to my left. I looked at him and then I turned to Jeanne and with my hands, I made a circle in front of me. I whispered to Jeanne, "He has such a big head." Why I whispered that to her instead of using my regular voice I do not know, but it didn't matter, because no sooner had I said it, I heard the words, "I heard you," coming from my left side.

I whipped my head to the left and looked straight at Rishi; he was looking right at me and I could see in his eyes that he had heard me and responded back to my rude comment about him.

I turned to Jeanne and said, "He heard me." She just chuckled and nodded her head, as if this was a daily occurrence in their home.

This was a first for me, the first time I had received anything from a cat, and the first time I had ever told anyone that I heard animals talking to me. I was trying to start a business and didn't want it getting around that I thought I was Dr. Doolittle, but it came out before I even realized what I was saying.

I also felt that nobody in this house was judging me and maybe they knew what I was talking about, and had more knowledge of what was happening than I did.

I firmly believe that events and people come into our lives so we can learn from them.

I watched Rishi many times after that first meeting when Jeanne had to be away from home. Jeanne and Rishi moved to another town, but I see them often and consider her a dear friend.

Okay, let's see if you have been following this story. Which Clair does it illustrate? If you said Clairaudience, you are right. As I have mentioned, Clairaudience, clear hearing, was the psychic sense that came through to me the strongest and the loudest in the beginning.

Since writing this chapter I received a text one night from Jeanne saying Rishi was very sick and the vet gave him maybe a week to ten days. Without a series of tests, they could not determine the source of his illness, but his kidneys were shutting down. Her concern was when would be the right time to let him cross over. I told Jeanne I would connect with Rishi and see if I could get any information for her.

I did connect with Rishi and I kept hearing the word tumor. He was very sick, and I told him that he was going to be in my book; he seemed excited about that. I received a little more from him and then we ended the connection.

I called Jeanne and explained what I knew the next morning, and when I told her about the book discussion, she said he went over to his dish that morning, ate a treat and seemed to be strutting around the house.

I told her to put his cat carrier on the floor and leave the door open and when he was ready to go to the vet he would enter his carrier. I also said to tell him it was okay to leave and that she did not want him to be in pain.

I talked to Jeanne about a week later and she said he had crawled into his carrier one day, after not drinking or eating for many days, and she knew it was time. He was letting her know he was ready to go to the vet.

Tigger

The next cat I remember having a conversation with was Tigger, and it was different, he used his voice to respond to me. I had been taking care of Tigger along with Chloe the dog while their pet parents, Kris and Curt, were away for a winter vacation. It was the third year of pet-sitting for them while they were on their annual winter vacation.

This one particular day I came into the garage. It was a finished garage, huge and heated, and Tigger greeted me by jumping up on a crate and watching while I prepared Chloe's food. I had let Chloe outside for her run and a potty break. Tigger ate dry food and wet food, with a choice of liver, turkey and fish, to be alternated daily.

I am always talking out loud to the animals, just like having a conversation with a friend.

This particular day the conversation went like this: "Tigger, what kind of food would you like today? Should we try some liver?"

To my surprise, Tigger vocally replied, "Liv-er," in his cat voice.

I was surprised by what I heard so I said, "Can you say liver?"

Tigger responded back, "Liv-er," again.

On my next visit, I brought my phone so I could record him if he did it again and if he didn't, it was just a fluke.

Tigger jumped up on the crate and I asked him again if he would like some liver and he replied, "Liv-er."

I still have the recording. I did try to get him to say turkey and he did his best, but it was a struggle.

He and I had a unique way of communicating, and he is the only animal who has spoken like that. Sure, some meow loudly and have unique voices, but he was the only one to try to form words.

That year was the last time I got to care for Tigger and Chloe; the next year their daughter moved into her own place and took the pets with her. I recently talked to Kris and she said that Tigger is no longer with us, but Chloe is still running around the house like her usual self.

The above story shows that if you talk to your pets and really listen to their responses, you might hear what they are saying to you. I have seen and heard dogs vocalize certain words and I have read they can have an IQ of a seven-year-old. When Tigger responded to my question with his vocalization, he knew I understood what he was saying by the look in his eyes and his body movement.

Marius

I received a message on my website one day from a woman by the name of Mary, wondering if I could take care of her daughter Erin's cat, and how did this pet-sitting thing work?

I called Mary and she explained they were going on a short trip, and the veterinarian had given them medication for Marius in pill form. She asked if I would be able to administer the pills. I said I could but I needed to meet Marius and get some information, and a time was set up for me to meet with Erin and Marius.

I don't know if you have ever had to give a pill to a cat, but it is not the same as giving one to a dog. With a dog, you can put it in a chunk of a hot dog, deli meat, a peanut-butter sandwich, or a piece of cheese and roll it into a ball, or even hide it in treats. Now they have something called "pill pockets," which is a treat with a hole in one end where you push in the pill and smoosh the end closed then hand it to them.

Antibiotics are usually a pill they will spit out if you don't disguise it in something tasty.

Cats are another story. You cannot hide it in their food, the pills have to be given orally and that is difficult to do. You do not want to be bitten; if you are, you probably need to get a shot. A cat bite is serious; it goes deep and has bacteria, something you don't want to mess with. You can try wrapping a bath towel around the cat so as not to get scratched, if they still have their claws. After a couple times of towel wrapping, if they see you have a towel, they hide. In 18 years of pet-sitting, I have never had an easy time getting a pill down a cat's throat.

Insulin shots are different. The animals seem to know they need it, and every cat that needed an insulin shot would be waiting for me to show up and let me inject the insulin with no resistance.

The day came to meet Erin and Marius. Mary waited outside to let me in. As we walked to Erin's apartment, she told me Marius was an older cat and not doing well, and it was hard to get the small pills down his throat.

I could see Marius perched on the back of the couch and sensed he was not doing well at all. Erin showed me where the litter box was, his food dishes and water bowl, and where the pills were kept. She also shared a little history of her life with Marius.

Mary showed me how tiny the pills were, I think they were in halves or maybe even fourths, and explained they were having a hard time keeping the pills in the pill shooter.

I suggested rubbing a little butter on the end of the pill shooter where the pill goes in to keep it in place and to get the pill to slide down Marius's throat at the same time.

I noticed they were coming at Marius to give him his pill. I showed them how to approach him from behind and place their thumb at one side of his mouth and the palm over the top of his head. With the middle finger on the other side of his mouth, to squeeze the corners of his mouth to open his mouth, and with the other hand insert the pill popper, push the plunger and the pill will go down his throat, if you're lucky.

As I was showing them this technique, I had my hand on Marius head and heard him say, "I don't want the pills, tell them I am ready to go. I am very sick."

This was the first time I had an animal tell me they were ready to go; the next time would be when my boy Shooz told me.

I sensed when I walked into the apartment that day, Marius's time here would not be much longer, but now he had asked me to let them know that. It was not a happy task before me; I would somehow have to tell them their cat had just said he was ready to leave this world.

I was at Erin's just before the weekend and they were not going to be leaving until the next week. They had been giving him the pills to see if they would help, if he would eat and drink more. As gently as I could, I explained to them that Marius was really sick as they had guessed and maybe he didn't want the pills because he thought they wouldn't help. I also said that Marius was an older cat and had a wonderful life with Erin. If he quit eating and drinking over the weekend they would probably have their answer, and when the time came to put Marius down they would know. But it would be sooner than later. When they did make that decision, I wanted them to know that Marius would still be with Erin.

Before I left that day, I told Marius what a magnificent cat he was and that it was an honor to have met him. When I walked out of the apartment I knew I would not see Marius again. My services would not be needed. A couple days later Mary called and said they would be taking Marius to the veterinarians to put him down. I again told her that Marius would be around Erin and she could talk to him any time she wished, and how sorry I was that they had to go through this. I give credit to Erin, she had a way with Marius, and they had their own communicating skills. But it is hard to make this decision when you are the pet parent.

Marius's story is about Clairsentience (clear feeling or clear sensing) and Clairaudience (clear hearing), when again more than one ability came through. This will happen as you develop your abilities, you may only use one or you may use more, it varies, depending on the situation.

Boomer And Gizzy

When Sherry called and asked me to explain my pet-sitting business to her, we talked quite a while on the phone. I answered most of her questions, then we set up a time for me to come for a meet-and-greet with the gang, and at the same time meet her and her husband Bob.

Sherry and Bob's family consisted of two cats, Boomer and Gizzy, and their dog Cinder. While Sherry explained their routine she also voiced her concern that Boomer had not been eating much and that she was afraid he would quit eating altogether for the four or five days they were gone. I assured her I would try to entice Boomer to eat, and that I had her phone number and the veterinarian's.

The first time I watched them I noticed Boomer did not eat much, maybe a few spoonful's of wet food, at the most. When I went back for the next visit Boomer would not eat at all and I decided to give him till the next time before I tried something different.

The next morning, I stopped by to let Cinder out and we walked around the backyard, came back inside, and I fed him. As I was getting the wet food ready for Boomer and Gizzy, I noticed that Boomer was up on a table. I set Gizzy's food down in the spot where she eats in the kitchen, and then took Boomer's food over to his spot on the floor where he eats.

As I was doing this, I asked nonchalantly, "What are you doing up there on the table?"

I heard back, "I want to eat up here."

I thought, okay, so I moved his food to the table and placed it in front of him and he wouldn't touch it. I was thinking, "Now what? He said he wants his food on the table, I put it up there and he is still not eating."

Then I knew what he needed. I took his small bowl and went to the cupboard where I found a small plate. I scraped his food onto the plate and set it down in front of him. He gave me a look that said, it took you long enough to figure it out, and began to eat. I then took what was left of Gizzy's food and put that on a plate for her. Boomer ate on the table from a plate for the rest of my visits.

What I all of a sudden realized was that Gizzy and Boomer are Persian cats and they have the breed's smooshed-up faces. When they put their faces down into the small bowls, the food was smeared all over their mouths and noses, making it hard for Boomer to eat and breathe. And when he was up on the table Cinder would not bother him.

Sherry called a couple days into their trip to see if Boomer was eating. I explained to her what I had done and that everyone was well.

I talked to Sherry four months later, and she shared with me that Boomer and Gizzy are still eating off the plates, no more bowls for them, and that Boomer is still eating on top of the table. He has not missed a meal and they are no longer worried about him.

The above story is about two abilities coming through but not at the same time. The first one, Clairaudience (clear hearing), was followed by Claircognizance (clear knowing), which helped me understand why Boomer was not eating after I did what he asked. Sometimes there is more than one answer to the issue. It's like an onion, you peel away one layer at a time.

CHAPTER SEVEN
FINDING THE LOST

In the past eighteen years of pet sitting I have had people call me with all kinds of questions and not all of them were about pet sitting. For example, my dog or cat is not acting right, I think it is sick, what would you recommend we do? I recommend that they take their pet to their veterinarian as I am not a vet. What do I think about certain foods, toys, and collars? I have found a lost pet, or I have lost a pet, what shall I do? My recommendations for a lost pet or if you have found a lost pet is to call the local radio station, check with the local humane society, or the city pound if there is one.

Also notify the local vet clinics, put up posters on corners and in gas stations, and the most important way to get the word out fast to a lot of people is Facebook. You might put an ad in the local newspaper with a reward for the return of your pet. If someone calls me with either situation I tell them to share it on my website or Facebook page. A dog can travel up to five miles a day when they are lost, especially if they are on the scent of a creature.

An example of this was a summer evening while I was out on

my dog rounds. I got a call from my neighbor saying she and her daughter had been on a walk and found a young St. Bernard dog down by the river, hiding in the tall grass. They said it seemed to be friendly but had no tags on the collar. They tried to give it water but it would not drink, probably because it was right next to a river.

I suggested they take a picture of the dog with their phone and send it to me so I could share it with my friends, and they did. I told them I would check on the dog as soon as I finished my dog rounds and bring it some food since it was right down the road from my house. We had an outdoor kennel the dog could sleep in for the night if the need arose.

When I got to the dog I could see it was a young dog and very hungry. While I was waiting for the dog to finish eating the food I had brought with me, the daughter texted me that she had found the owner and he was on the way. He had seen her post on Facebook. I also found out the dog had been missing about five days and lived thirty-five miles away from where he ended up, by the river.

I always suggest a collar for your dog on which you can write your phone number with a black "sharpie" marker. It seems more often than not if dogs have tags on their collars with information, the tags always seem to be gone when the dog is found. If the collar is still on the dog, the phone number is also there for anybody to see.

Another thing I hear is the dog is micro-chipped and all that information is on the chip. That is wonderful if the person finding the animal takes the time to bring it to where the chip can be read. Some people know nothing about micro-chips and we should have more public awareness. I suggest to those who find a pet that they take it to their vet or local shelter to determine if it is chipped.

As the years went by I got more and more calls about lost pets, and I gave them the same advice until one day when I got a call about Boomer.

Boomer

One cold, wet, sleeting morning in early spring I received a frantic call from Cari and Mike. I had taken care of their family pets before: Milo an older Pug, Faith an older Sheepdog Terrier mix, and Lily a Chihuahua and Pug mix. But Cari was calling this time because her daughter Jackie's dog Boomer, a Shiatzu and Poodle mix puppy, had bolted out the door before they could stop him. Cari and Mike walked and drove the neighborhood looking for Boomer but had not seen him. Cari called me wanting to know if I had any suggestions for her.

I told her the usual things to do and then something nudged me to tell her that maybe I could connect with Boomer. I explained to her briefly what that meant. I was not sure how she would react, but when you are frantically searching for a pet, you might be game for anything. Cari was willing to see if I could receive anything and I was nervous about trying. This was my first official attempt at communicating with a pet that was lost, and all sorts of things were going through my head like: "Who do you think you are?" You're not going to get anything." "That animal is not going to talk to you." "It is all in your head."

What I found out later is that those doubts I was hearing were my ego talking, and ego did not want me to do this, since it would create change. Ego was happy with the way things were, and feared the unknown. Ego is there to protect you against uncertainty.

I told Cari I would give it a try. I went into my basement where it was quiet and shut the door. With no noise to distract me (I would think this was necessary for a long time), I took some deep breaths in and out and grounded myself. In the best interest of all involved, I would try to help bring Boomer home.

To the west of Cari and Mike's house is a small river and on the other side of the river is more housing and a street with the name Garnet. When I talked to Cari earlier, I had told her to go towards Garnet, maybe Boomer was in that neighborhood. Why I thought Boomer was over in that direction I did not know.

When I tried to connect with Boomer the words I received were river and underbrush. When you communicate, it might be with words, it might be partial sentences, but you need to trust what you get. I called Cari back and told her I had heard the words river and underbrush, so she hung up and went to look for Boomer.

Cari called back shortly after speaking with me. Mike and she had found Boomer down by the river; he was caught in some underbrush and was soaking wet and shivering but okay. I suggested she call her veterinarian to see what they advised, since he was a puppy. Cari heated towels in her dryer and wrapped them around Boomer, and the little escape artist was just fine, although I think it was awhile before Jackie was told about his escape.

Milo is no longer with us and greatly missed, Faith has gotten older and lives in her own little world, and Lily has calmed down and watches over Faith.

Cari called me one other time about a missing dog. I had forgotten about it until she reminded me when I was asking her about the above story. The reason I had forgotten was my dad had been in the hospital with complications from his cancer. This time when she called I could not go to my quiet zone, I was in a hospital with what seemed like chaos around me, and I had a lot on my mind.

As she was explaining that they had been looking for this dog for quite a while, I told her to stay put, don't go looking, stay where you are, the dog will come to you. I had received this right there on the spot and did not think any more of it. I did not know how I had this knowledge; it was just there in my mind.

Cari called me back and told me they had done exactly what I said to do, and soon the dog was back at their side.

In both stories I had not met either dog and the information I received in the first story was Clairaudience (clear hearing). and in the second story it was received by Claircognizance (clear knowing). This would be the start of my work to find lost pets and overcome my ego as it tried to protect me by keeping me in my safety zone.

Cookie

The next call I would receive was from Christie about her dog Cookie, who was missing from her yard, but her other dog Frodo hadn't left. Frodo is a Pomeranian and Pekingese mix and has been with a Christie a long time. Cookie, an Australian Shepherd and German Short-haired pointer mix, was the newest addition to Christie's family. According to Christie, both dogs had been in her yard and when she went to let them in, she discovered Cookie was gone. Christie said she had been out looking for Cookie for a day now, when someone suggested she call me to ask if I could help her locate Cookie. When Christie called, I told her I would try to help with Cookie when I finished my pet rounds.

I was finally able to sit down and quiet my mind to see if I could connect with Cookie. Now when I say connect, it sounds like an easy thing to do, as if the animals start chatting about where they are and what's around them, but there is a little more to it than that. I will describe this process in a later chapter at the end of the book.

I was shown a small shed, a tree, grass, and an owl, and I felt Cookie was close to Christie's house. I called Christie, who had been out driving in search of Cookie, with others looking as well, but they'd had no luck. I told her what I had received from Cookie and to go outside and listen for an owl and to keep in touch.

I believe it was on a Monday that Christie contacted me the first time and it was toward the end of the week when she called to tell me that Cookie had been found. I could tell in Christie's voice that something was wrong and she said that Cookie was in intensive care at an emergency veterinarian clinic. Cookie was fighting for her life.

Minnesota is the land of ten thousand lakes, and if you live by a lake it's on a parcel of land called a lake lot. Christie lived by a lake and near her house was a lot with a small camper. The people who owned it usually came down for the weekend. Somehow when the owners of the camper left that Sunday night Cookie got locked in the camper without anybody knowing. The camper had packets of mouse poison called D-Con and Cookie had eaten some. D-Con is not good for any animal; it shuts down their organs, and that's what was happening to Cookie.

Between Christie's house and the lot with the camper lived an elderly gentleman who was hard of hearing, and never heard Cookie barking next door. I don't know if it was the elderly man who eventually spotted Cookie or the owners of the camper, but when they opened the door Cookie was lying there and Christie rushed her to the vet and then to the emergency veterinarian hospital. Cookie did pull through and is a happy, healthy girl, but it was a close call.

I saw Christie about a month or so after Cookie was found and she told me she went inside that camper. It had only one small window, and when she looked out she saw a small shed, a tree, and a plastic owl on top of the shed. It was the same information I had received from Cookie.

The lesson I learned from Cookie was that when I told Christie to go outside and listen for an owl hooting, it was my twist on trying to make sense of what I was getting from Cookie. Now I report exactly what I am given and only that, it is not up to me to try to make sense of anything the animals tell me. Part of this story is about Clairvoyance (clear seeing), and Clairsentience (clear feeling), when I felt that Cookie was near Christie's house.

Daisy and Dotty

I received a call from Sandy who had some questions about my pet-sitting service because she was going to be out of town and wanted her pets to stay at home. We made an appointment for me to come to her house to do a meet-and-greet with the gang. Sandy's family of pets consisted of Toby and Buddy, who are Golden retrievers, and Daisy and Dotty, who are Basset Hounds.

The day came for me to go meet the crew and they were a great bunch of dogs. I was given the pertinent information and instructions and the days and times I would be coming. A few days later Sandy called me to tell me Daisy and Dotty were missing. Sandy had let them out that morning like she always does, but while she was getting ready for work, they had taken off. She figured a critter had come into the yard and they followed it, because they never left her yard.

I had just met Sandy but I wanted to do all I could to help get her dogs back home. So, I put aside my ego, which was telling me you can't tell her you talk to dogs, what will she think, and said, "Sometimes I can connect with dogs to see if they can show or tell me something. Would I have your permission to try?" It was quiet on the other end of the phone, and my ego was telling me, you blew that one, when Sandy replied, "Sure, go ahead and try."

Later that day I was able to get home to my quiet zone and try to connect with Daisy and Dotty, and when I did I felt I was only getting information from one of them, but they were together. The information I received from whomever, was a picture of a lake and tall grasses. I called Sandy with this and told her I would check back the next day.

She went down the road to a nearby lake on the way to her house and drove around but she did not find them. I called her the next day and she told me they had no luck around the lake and I promised to connect with the dogs again, but felt they were north of her house.

It would be later that day before I was able to quiet my mind and communicate with the dogs. The information I received was of the water and tall grasses again, but something new was added, and at the same time I felt I was receiving from both dogs. The addition was a picture of two blue silos on a farm. They're technically called Harvestore silos, and they are different from the older cement silos.

I called Sandy and asked if there were any Harvestore silos nearby. She said there was a farm a few miles north of their house with Harvestor silos and she would send her daughter over there. I told her they were not at that farm because I was seeing the silos from a distance. The search party should take the vehicle they always drive because dogs can recognize the sound of a familiar vehicle up to a mile away.

Her daughter drove to the farm and the dogs were not there as I said they would not be, since they were showing me the silos from a distance. A few hours later they drove back up to the farm and turned around and on the way back home they found the dogs walking along the side of the road.

Sandy called me, saying they had found them. They were tired, dirty, and their noses were scraped up from following trails, but otherwise they were in good shape.

About a month later I had some time and decided to go see if I could find the place that Daisy and Dotty had shown me when they were missing. I needed verification that these were not just lucky guesses like my ego was telling me, even though I knew better.

I drove up to Sandy's house and then continued north on that road when all of a sudden I saw the lake the dogs had sent me, a man-made lake by the Department of Natural Resources, and alongside the lake was the field of tall grasses. As I looked north, in the distance were the two blue Harvestor silos, and I was elated.

I believe both dogs communicated with me, especially the second time I connected with them, but being new at this I did not ask which one I was hearing from.

It was also the first time I had seen something in the distance and knew that it meant they were not there but looking at it from farther away.

I had also received in the second message that they were hot and tired, but to me that was obvious so I did not mention it to Sandy.

I spoke with Sandy recently and learned that Daisy and Dotty are just fine, and so are Toby and Buddy, but she did say they had a fence built around their yard.

There are three Clair's in this story: Clairvoyance (clear seeing), with the silos, tall grasses and the lake; Clairsentience (clear feeling), when I felt the dogs were north of her house and still together; and Claircognizance (clear knowing), when I knew that the dogs were seeing the silos from a distance, in that field of tall grasses by the lake.

Angel

My friend Johanne and her husband Francis are animal lovers, and have cats, horses, and many dogs. This wonderful couple has visited the local Humane Society many times and adopted the older dogs nobody seems to want. They bring them home to their horse ranch to live out their days. Their pet family when I first met them consisted of Mr. Magoo, a chocolate lab; Koumo, a Black Lab, Golden retriever mix; and Cody, a German Shorthaired Pointer. Then along came Maya, another Chocolate Lab; and Nanouk, a German Shorthaired Pointer.

The family included the following older dogs they had adopted as they became available: Buford, a Basset Hound; Pepper, a Black (you guessed it) Miniature Poodle; Koho, a Chesapeake Bay Retriever; Izzy, a Great Pyrenees (next story); Angel, a white Toy Poodle who was blind and slightly deaf; and Sid, who was a Black Lab who when they adopted was riddled with cancer and very sick. Sid only lived two weeks after they brought him into their home but at least he died in a place that was full of love for animals and not in the shelter alone.

Johanne and Francis did not have all these pets at once, some of their own and some of the adopted members have passed over the years. When this happens, another pet will join the group. The two newest additions are Benny, a Chocolate Lab puppy; and LoLou, a Black Lab and Pointer mix puppy.

It was a late evening in February when I received a text from Johanne that she and her husband Francis were in Mexico for a mid-winter vacation, and there was a problem with one of her dogs. Because of the needs of the horse ranch, Johanne had a gal staying at their house to care for the horses and the rest of the animals.

The problem was Angel somehow got out of the house when nobody was looking, and her being blind and deaf did not help. Since it was February in Minnesota, the ground was covered with snow and it dropped below zero at night, sometimes to thirty below zero.

The girl and her boyfriend had searched that afternoon and evening but could not find Angel. So, Johanne had called me to see if I could check with Angel.

It was eleven o'clock at night my time and I told her I would try to connect with Angel in the morning and help look for her as soon as I finished my dog rounds.

I quieted my mind the next morning, I like to call it "zeroing out," and tried to connect with Angel. I did receive some information, not much and not for very long, Angel showed me that she had been going in circles in the snow not knowing where she was (remember, she was blind and was using her sense of smell to find her way), and then I heard the word EXHAUSTED.

The next thing I received I had never experienced before, my connection went black. I saw the black screen of a television, and knew she was no longer with us. The reason I had never been given this picture was the animals were alive when I was trying to get them home. I was being shown Angel was no longer here physically.

Since this was a new experience for me I still went over to Johanne's that morning to look for Angel. We had a small snowfall the night before so I looked for new tiny tracks but never found any. I also let the big dogs out to go with me on my search, with no luck.

I returned to town to do my noon pet rounds and then came back to Johanne's that afternoon to search. Angel was never found. I have not checked in with Angel since that day but someday I will to see if she has anything more for us to bring peace of mind to Johanne and Francis.

Most of this story is about Clairvoyance (clear seeing); when I heard the word exhausted it was Clairaudience (clear hearing); and the blank television screen was both Clairvoyance, to see, and Claircognizance (clear knowing), to know that she was gone. The pets currently with Johanne and Francis are: Maya (the oldest); Nanouk; and Benny and LoLou, the last two puppies. They will have their hands full for a while.

Izzy

Unlike the other stories in this chapter, Izzy, a Great Pyrenees, was not lost, she was dumped along a road and the car was seen driving off. This happened at the end of August and the weather was still nice. Izzy wandered to the local county transfer station (landfill) where there is quite a bit of acreage and the property is fenced and the gates are locked at night.

The workers at the landfill took a liking to Izzy and started feeding her part of their lunches and made sure she had fresh water every day, but she did not let anyone get too close.

Izzy had a daily routine. She would wander out to see the guys working with pay-loaders and trucks then circle back to the offices, and in the afternoon, she would go to the quiet spot behind the buildings and take her nap.

The local Humane Society sent some staff and volunteers over to try and catch Izzy, but to no avail. That is when Johanne (from the previous story), who was a Humane Society board member and my friend, decided to call me to see if I could help catch Izzy. It was the first week in September when I got the call and I said I would try.

I suggested we take Johanne's dogs Maya and Koumo out with us to coax her into the truck. Johanne's dogs are super-friendly but Izzy wanted nothing to do with us. I decided then that I needed to earn the Big Girl's trust (I called her that because she didn't have a name at the time), knowing any sudden grabs would get us nowhere and that this was going to be a slow process.

I would go out to see Izzy at the landfill four to six times a week in-between my afternoon dog rounds and my early evening dog rounds. I started out by walking to wherever the workers had last spotted her to toss hamburgers and hot dogs to her, but she was not interested.

So, I started bringing packets of dog food that look like hamburger to leave a trail on the ground. Then I would sit off in the distance and talk softly to her as she would slowly follow the trail, watching from the corner of her eye for any sudden movement from me.

After about a week, she started to follow me, keeping her distance, while I would drop dog treats as we walked the landfill grounds. All the while I was carrying on a conversation with her so she would become accustomed to my voice.

Finally, Izzy would take the treats from my hand, her eyes on my other hand for movement, and if she saw any perceived threat she would back away. I noticed that her eyes looked like an older dog's, but her teeth looked like a younger dog's.

It was November fourth when Izzy was finally caught and taken to a local boarding place, Rolling Acres, because the local Humane Society shelter was full. I kept working with Izzy while she was at Rolling Acres; she was now confined to an indoor/outdoor run and I was able to leash her and take her on walks. I was also able to pet her, careful not to overdo it.

I continued to bring her treats and was now feeding her large cans of wet dog food mixed with dry. I was hoping this would put on weight since she was all fur and bones.

It was Thanksgiving weekend and as I approached her kennel I was talking to her and she started to wag her tail. I was elated, it was such a simple gesture, but she had not wagged her tail the whole three months I had been working with her. Izzy had finally accepted me.

That next week there was an opening at the local Humane Society so Johanne and I took her to a local groomer. Amanda volunteered to bathe and groom Izzy. After Amanda got all the loose hair and tangles out and gave Izzy a nice bath, Johanne went to pick her up and take her to the shelter, but seeing her all clean and brushed, Johanne decided to take Izzy home to foster her.

When Johanne and Francis say they are going to foster a dog, it really means they will be adopting that dog, and that is what happened with Izzy. Izzy was taken to the vet: she weighed eighty pounds, underweight for a dog of her breed and size; she was between three and five years old; and probably had birthed two or three litters of puppies.

Izzy would only be at Johanne and Francis's home for about two months. Great Pyrenees dogs are a working class of dogs, and are bred to watch over and guard sheep, as well as herd goats.

Johanne's dogs soon got tired of being herded, and one day while Johanne was in town on errands, Izzy decided to mosey across the road to the turkey farm. While she was there she began herding the turkeys.

It did not go well. Johanne ended up with a bill for the turkeys that did not make it after Izzy's visit. Izzy needed to go to where she could do what her breed does best.

Johanne did some research and found a Great Pyrenees rescue group with the perfect home for Izzy. Johanne took her to Minneapolis where a mutual friend transported Izzy the rest of the way to her home in Iowa, where Izzy met her new pet family.

The last I heard from Johanne, Izzy was in charge of the abandoned Great Pyrenees pups that came to the rescue ranch, and was in seventh heaven watching over them.

I fostered a Great Pyrenees named Betty for about six months before my nephew Travis took her home. Shortly after Betty arrived, Travis got a Black Lab puppy and Betty guarded that puppy with her life.

One day some coyotes wandered into his yard and tried to grab the puppy. Unbeknownst to the coyotes, it would be the last thing they did. Betty heard the puppy yelping and before Travis could grab his gun to shoot the coyotes, Betty had already clamped down on each marauder and with a swift shake she broke their necks. The point being, this breed takes their work seriously.

Izzy's story is one with Claircognizance. I knew it would be a long process to gain Izzy's trust, and that at the same time, she was a gentle dog and would not harm me. How I knew this, I did not know, I just did.

CHAPTER EIGHT
END OF LIFE WITH YOUR PET

This chapter is hard to write. It speaks to pet owners whose pets have come to the end of their journey in life. Between the twenty years of my house-cleaning business and the eighteen years of pet-sitting, I have been present with many owners whose pets had to be euthanized, and to put it mildly, it SUCKS!!!

I have accompanied my clients and their pets so they would not have to face this time alone. I have taken pets to the vet and stayed with them when their pet parents could not, when it was a pet I had watched. It never gets easier and there is always a box of Kleenex waiting for me. I believe that an animal I have cared for, whether it's mine or a client's, deserves to have someone with them when they pass from this physical world or, as some people say, "cross the rainbow bridge." They have been faithful through all your ups and downs; you can at least be at their side for this end-of-life passage when they need you. It will never be easy, and there will be many tears, but when it is all over you will know in your heart you made the right choice to be with them.

Gracie

Gracie was a Golden Retriever and lived with her family, George, Liz and Lily the cat. When I started pet-sitting for them Gracie was already an older dog. Gracie had dealt with a bout of Lyme's Disease and her front legs were almost stiff from the effects of this disease; it was similar to arthritis, and she would walk with a stiff gait in her front legs.

Gracie loved pheasant hunting and would go with George every year, some years more than once. Gracie knew when the season started to change and it would be hunting time again.

When George and Liz would go on trips, I would watch Gracie and Lily. Gracie had a routine she never deviated from. Like most animals, her morning consisted of taking the same route for the same amount of time, and then she would come back inside for breakfast.

I remember it was a fall evening close to Halloween when Gracie and I were out for her evening walk. As we were heading down the road in this rural neighborhood, I saw something off to my right that looked like a big dog. Now, it was dark and I had a flashlight with me, but there were also street lights on.

I told Gracie, "It looks like we have company," and kept walking. This big dog kept coming towards us and then I realized it was not a dog but a small deer. In fact, it was a small buck (male deer) with a nice rack of horns. What happened next is strange and I could tell it was making Gracie nervous because she picked up her pace.

The buck started walking along beside us, so close I could touch him. In fact, I did touch him as I tried to push him away but he would not leave us. So now all three of us were walking down the road side by side, long before cell phones were available, as otherwise I would have taken a video of this.

My guess was this deer was raised by humans or there was something wrong with him. The sad reality was that deer hunting season was a week away and as friendly as he was, he would walk up to a hunter and with that beautiful rack, he would be shot. Even though he was a small deer he would be an easy target.

As we came upon a house I decided to see if he belonged to them or if they knew anything about this deer.

Gracie and I went up the three steps and onto their porch and as I was ringing the doorbell Gracie was shoving me. I looked down at Gracie and the deer was coming up the last step to join us.

Nobody answered the door so I managed to get the deer, Gracie and myself off their porch and back down the road.

As we continued to the next house, which had lights on, I saw in their yard fake, ceramic life-sized deer. I rang the doorbell, looked over my shoulder and saw the buck standing in the yard with the deer. I felt so bad for him; he wanted to belong so desperately.

A young gal answered the door, I asked her if she knew anything about the deer and she said "no." I think she was glad to see us go, she seemed a little nervous.

Gracie and I returned to her house and the last I ever saw of that deer was him standing with the fake deer in the yard. I asked Liz about it after they got back and she said she saw him in the summer, but after hunting season, nobody saw him again.

After thinking about this young buck years later, I realized that even wild animals need to be appreciated during their time here with us.

I continued to look after Gracie when George and Liz would take a trip. It was getting harder for Gracie to go pheasant hunting. Although her heart was still in it, her body was telling her otherwise. George decided to get another dog so Gracie could show the ropes to this puppy.

That is where Tillie came into the family. Tillie is a Gordon Setter and very colorful, in more ways than one.

I don't remember if it was January or February when George and Liz left on vacation, but it was very, very cold. The dogs would be in the house and could also be in the garage, if they wanted, for a short while and sometimes Gracie liked to sit out there.

In the garage was a huge wooden crate with blankets inside and draped over the sides, along with dog beds. George and Liz had been gone a couple days and on this particular morning, after feeding Gracie and Tillie, we had taken our walk and come back to their house.

Gracie decided she wanted to be in the garage, so of course Tillie did too. I left them out there and left for the rest of my dog stops. I would be back at noon to let them out again for a walk and put them in back the house.

About two hours later I got this nagging feeling to go back and check on Gracie, not Tillie and Gracie, just Gracie. I did not know why, but the feeling kept getting stronger so I drove to Gracie's house.

When I got there a car was in the driveway and I figured it was their cleaning person, so I went into the garage where Gracie was lying in the farthest corner.

I entered the house to let the cleaning lady know I was there so she wouldn't be startled, and stepped back into the garage. Gracie was not getting up to greet me, and sometimes it was hard for her, but she was not moving, just looking at me.

As I walked toward Gracie I saw a microwave on the floor out of the corner of my eye. It was one of the first ones they made, those huge, heavy, Amana microwaves and it had been sitting on top of the blanket on the crate.

I looked back at Gracie and knew instantly what had happened. Gracie had been lying by the crate on a blanket, Tillie came along, and being the puppy that she is, started to pull on the blanket, toppling the microwave onto Gracie.

In her elderly years with Lyme's and arthritis, Gracie could not have moved out of the way in time. When I got to Gracie I saw her front leg was swollen and when I tried to stand her up she couldn't put weight on it. I immediately called their vet and explained what happened and said I was bringing Gracie in.

I went into the house and got the cleaning lady to help me load Gracie into my vehicle, put Tillie in the house and was on my way to the vet clinic. As I was driving I called Liz to tell her about the accident and that I would be in touch after I talked to the vet.

Dr. Tom was a friend of George and Liz's and he knew Gracie well; he was also a hunter. He took x-rays and saw that her leg was shattered and the other was very swollen. In order to fix this Gracie would have to endure a four-hour trip to the university of veterinary, and would end up with a rod in her leg. Being elderly, she would be at risk when going under anesthesia for the surgery.

Dr. Tom said he would call Liz and George and discuss this with them. I told him to assure them if they chose to put Gracie down I would be with her.

George and Liz had previously discussed Gracie's health concerns with Dr. Tom. When he called with the results of the x-rays and explained the difficulty Gracie would have walking with the rod in her leg, if she survived the surgery, and that it would not be a good result for her, the choice was made to end her life.

I went into a room and they brought Gracie to me. I told her as I was holding her, bawling my eyes out, that I loved her, her family loved her and she was a beautiful, wonderful companion and hunter. It was an honor for me to have been her pet sitter, but it was ok for her to let go and I gave her a big kiss, and then she was gone.

Dr. Tom gave me a hug and said this was best for Gracie. He then handed me a Kleenex.

That was a turning point. I was the strong one, I never cried at funerals, never cried in public, but here I was sobbing my eyes out over my bond with Gracie and I didn't care if anyone saw me. It would not be the only time at this vet clinic they would witness this scene, there would be more.

I finally left the clinic and got into my vehicle, and now I had to call Liz and George. Even though they knew what had been decided, I had to tell them.

It was so hard for them not to be there for their longtime companion and say their final goodbyes. I felt so bad for them and they were feeling bad for me that I had to do this.

I took Gracie's collar and leash back to the house and checked on Tillie. This was in the beginning of my intuitive abilities so I never considered sitting Tillie down and explaining to her where Gracie was. In fact, I never thought about that until Midnite passed away and I told Shooz. Now I recommend telling any animals still at home why the deceased pet is not coming home, because when you left with that pet they probably already knew it was sick or something was wrong.

I talked to the cleaning lady later that day to let her know what had been decided about Gracie and to thank her for helping me load Gracie into my vehicle.

She told me she had heard a loud crack that morning but thought it was so cold out that the house was adjusting; they sometimes do that in very cold weather. What she actually heard was the loud noise of the microwave hitting the floor in the garage.

I continued to care for Tillie and Lily until George and Liz arrived. I expressed my sorrow to them over their loss. I continue to pet sit for them, Tillie is still around and they've acquired another cat, Odie. Eventually they had to put Lily down. Now it's just Tillie and Odie. Odie is very vocal, and Tillie lives for the hunting season.

This story is about Clairsentience (clear feeling), when I got the nagging feeling I had to check on Gracie; Claircognizance (clear knowing), when I knew what happened with the microwave; and Clairvoyance (clear seeing), because I saw a picture of Tillie pulling on the blanket and knocking the microwave off the crate onto Gracie.

Unknown Dog

It was a November night and I was on my early evening dog rounds driving around the lake, when I spotted something what looked like a black garbage bag in the middle of the road. As I went by I saw that it was a dog.

I turned around, drove back to the spot and pulled over on the side of the road. As I was getting out of my vehicle, I saw a man running down his driveway and a woman who had stopped and was out of her car and walking toward us.

The dog was bleeding from his head and mouth. The man said it was his dog, the woman said she had hit the dog with her car and it should not have been in the road. Some compassion.

I suggested we get the dog out of the middle of the road since it was dark and we did not want to be hit next. The woman left, saying she had things to do.

I ran back to my vehicle and grabbed a blanket to put under the dog so we could lift it out of the middle of the road and onto their lawn. I then asked the man the name of his veterinarian and he said Dr. Tom.

I called Dr. Tom's cell phone number since it was after hours and I told him that a dog had been hit on the road. He asked if it was mine and I told him it was not. He then asked who it belonged to. I told him I did not know the owners name, so I asked the gentleman his name and he replied, "Michael."

It turned out Dr. Tom's daughter and Michael's daughter were both in Chicago together for a school function.

Dr. Tom said he would meet us at the vet clinic, which for us was about five minutes away. Michael said we could load the dog into his vehicle. I climbed in the back and held the dog wrapped in the blanket while he drove. On the way to the vet clinic I talked softly to the dog as it was bleeding.

We reached the vet clinic before Dr. Tom, and just as he was pulling into the driveway the dog died in my arms. I knew he was gone.

Dr. Tom and Michael carried him into the vet clinic where he examined him and confirmed that the dog had died. Dr. Tom assured us the dog had been brain dead as soon as he was hit and did not feel a thing. It didn't lessen the sadness I felt for Michael and his family.

I left Dr. Tom and Michael to get some fresh air and think about what had just happened. Michael came out and we drove the five minutes back to his house. When we got out, I gave him a hug and said I was so sorry for him and his family and left to go back to my dog stops with blood all over my clothes.

That was a tough night for me. I kept thinking about the family and their dog and what a tragedy that death was.

About a week later, I was home one night and a vehicle pulled into my driveway. A man and woman got out and it was Michael and his wife Betsy with a gift of appreciation for me. It was an angel in silver with a dog in its arms, bearing the caption, Guardian of Animals. I have kept it to this day.

They told me that night Betsy was out running with the dog. I asked his name and they said Kobe. He was a Black Lab they had rescued. While they were standing in their driveway, Kobe spotted something, ran into the road and the woman hit their dog. Betsy raced to the house to get Michael and that is when I came into the picture. Their other daughter who was home at the time looked in my vehicle for any identification after we left for the vet clinic. She told her mom I was okay because the seat covers were covered with paw prints.

Michael and Betsy would adopt two more dogs, brothers, a Black Lab and Golden Retriever mix, and they reminded me of my dog Midnite. Their names were Apollo and Bode. I would learn this when I was asked to become their pet sitter.

I got to know the family, and also became a pet sitter for Michael's sisters MaryBeth and her husband Hans, and their family of dogs and peacocks; and Jean and her husband Jim, and their family of dogs. Bode and Apollo were well-behaved for dogs their size and friendly; they loved their walks by the lake.

Michael and Betsy would move to the other side of the lake where Apollo and Bode explored the woods in their backyard. I loved to come and pet-sit for them.

One day Michael told me that Apollo had bone cancer in his back leg and it could not be treated. Apollo was a trooper and he went through many months of limping, but eventually he was so weak and ill, the decision was made to put him down.

I happened to see Michael on a service road where he flagged me down. He said Apollo was in the back seat of the truck if I wanted to say goodbye. I walked up to the window and Apollo stuck his head out. I gave him a hug and kissed him on his head, and told him how much I loved him, and what an honor it was to have known him. I said it was ok to let go and walked away from the truck with tears in my eyes. I got into my vehicle and cried all the way to my next dog stop.

Bode is still doing great; he has had difficulty with his leg as he is older now, and still afraid of storms, but is always happy to see me, as I am to see him.

This story is about Claircognizance (clear knowing). I knew what I needed to do and I knew the instant the dog died in my arms. At the time, I did not know anything about Clair's and just attributed it to gut instinct. I now know it was this form of intuition.

Flash

Flash was a rescued Basset Hound in the pet family of Paul and Beth mentioned in chapter four. Flash was middle-aged but he easily fit in with the rest of the crew. Flash always had an opinion and he voiced it often. If Beth was at a meeting out of town and he had to be picked up from the groomers or the vet clinic, I would be there for Flash.

As soon as I would get him into my vehicle and start down the road, I would ask him, "What do you think?" He would tell me in his deep Basset voice all the way to his house. I have a few videos of this I have kept on my phone.

When Beth and Paul were to be gone for more than a week they would have a friend of Beth's from another town stay with the dogs and keep an eye on things, but in an emergency I was the back-up.

Paul and Beth had been overseas for about three weeks when I got a text from Beth early one morning saying her friend called saying Flash had been throwing up all night and was not doing well. She would be taking him to the vet as soon as she could get them to return her call. Beth wanted to know if I could meet her friend and Flash there.

I said I would, I had one more dog stop, and asked her to let me know what time she was going. Her friend got the call back from the vet, and she was to meet him in fifteen minutes. I was done with my dog stops for the morning and I went to join her.

When I got to the vet clinic they were already inside, and Flash was on the table and did not look good. I went over to the table and called his name. He lifted his head and I said, "Flash, you are one sick boy."

He looked me in the eye and I knew he was at his end of life. The vet said they would run a blood test and give him some fluids with pain medication intravenously. Beth's friend said she had to go to work but would be back in town around four o'clock.

I knew Flash could not last that long and told the vet I would be around if needed, and that I would be back before noon. When I left, I sent Beth a message that Flash was very sick and had lost weight and that the vet would be contacting her.

It was an hour and a half later when Beth called and asked if I could help Flash cross over. The clinic told her he was in a lot of pain and crying. I told her I would be on my way as soon as we hung up.

When I got to the clinic Flash was lying on a blanket on the floor with tubes in him and I sat down beside him so I could put his head in my lap and pet him. While I held his head, I told him that his family and I loved him so much, that he was a wonderful dog and it was a privilege to know him.

The vet asked if I was ready and I reluctantly said yes. I gave him a kiss from Beth and one from me and told him it was ok to let go, we understood it was time, and then he was gone, no longer in distress.

Lost in tears, I knew this was best for him, but it was so hard, knowing Beth and Paul would have wanted to say goodbye to Flash if it had been at all possible.

Claircognizance (clear knowing) was present here, when I saw Flash and knew he was near the end. You might also say it was Clairsentience (clear feeling). What is the difference? I knew, how I knew I didn't know, but I also knew I would be back before noon to help Flash cross over. It was not a feeling that I might be back, I knew I would be back, and I felt his sense of being really sick.

Lily

Lily was lucky to find a home with Terry, Michelle and their daughter Samantha. Lily was an older Pug, black in color (actually, she was more of a gray because of her age), and had been found in a field by a friend. The friend knew Terry and Michelle loved

Pugs and their two Pugs Nikki and Norman were no longer with them. They had adopted an all-black cat named Gus who was still around when they had Nikki. Gus as a kitten learned to hold his tail curled over his back like a Pug, and would come when you called him like a dog. I think he thought he was a Pug.

Gus once crawled into a heating vent on a summer day when the cover was off and ended up down by the furnace, then crawled up into the suspended ceiling in their basement. He learned to walk by their new faucet in the kitchen and it would automatically turn the water on; he just never learned to shut it off.

Gus was there to meet Lily when she came into her new home, and Gus was bigger than Lily but they would soon become friends.

Lily had a unique walk; she was bow-legged and it gave her a distinctive gait. She wasn't very big but she would melt your heart. Lily's hearing wasn't the best and her eyes were starting to fail, but she managed to get around and when she was determined to go somewhere, she was fast.

Lily got away from the house one day. Terry and Michelle looked for her but could not find Lily. The neighbor called them one evening and told them they had found Lily in a basement window well. Her eyes not being the best she had tumbled into it and could not get out. The neighbor's daughter had heard rustling sounds by her window and looked out to see Lily.

I could visit Lily regularly because Terry and Michelle had been my house-cleaning and pet-sitting clients. In the last couple years I could see Lily was aging and her health was deteriorating; she was developing a breathing issue, and her legs would give out every now and then, all typical of an aging dog.

In the meantime, Gus was also getting sick and he developed a pancreatic illness, which they tried to treat with medication but eventually had to put Gus to sleep, a sad day for the family. We would all miss him.

Terry, Michelle and Samantha went on a winter ski trip and as usual I would be taking care of Lily. I was excited to see her because after I quit the cleaning business, the only time I spent time with Lily was when they took a trip.

The weather we had been having was very cold, our nights were getting down to thirty below zero and the days were staying at about twenty below zero. It's what we Minnesotans call a cold snap. Dogs don't like to go out in this weather and I never blamed them, since I don't like it either.

When it was cold like that Michelle had me let Lily out on the deck, so she would not have to go down steps and be out very long. I would carry Lily out, set her on the path shoveled in the snow, and she would take care of her bathroom needs then run back up the steps and into the house.

The second morning I was there to let Lily out I opened the door to the deck and she went outside. As she was coming back in she fell over and collapsed. I bent down and scooped her up and was inside the house in one step. I set her on the floor, all the while asking her, "Lily, are you okay? Lily, hang in there. Lily, don't do this to me."

She sat up and walked away, struggling to breathe as she went. It was then I knew she had just fainted. I had never had a dog do that before and it was new to me. I also knew it was because she was not getting enough oxygen.

I called Michelle and she told me that Lily had done this once before, after she had climbed the stairs to the bedrooms.

I got Lily situated in her room on her dog bed, and she seemed to be breathing as normally as she could for her condition. I told her I would be back at lunchtime, gave her a dog treat and left.

During Lily's noon visit she fainted again; this time her breathing was more labored and her tongue was turning purple. I texted Michelle that I would take Lily to their vet.

The vet decided to take x-rays of Lily's chest and abdomen. Lily sat on my lap in the exam room while we waited. I tried to get Lily to calm down so her breathing would be easier. I knew the results would not be good, but was hoping otherwise.

The vet came into the room with the x-rays. Lily was full of fluids and had white spots all over her lungs. I explained that the family would not be home for another three days and she suggested pills to remove some of the fluids and another pill to help with breathing. The vet also said this was only a temporary fix until the family could get home, and might not be effective.

I took Lily home and tried to contact Michelle, but she was not answering so I tried Terry instead. When he answered I relayed what the vet prescribed.

Terry would talk to Michelle, and in the meantime, I sent Michelle a picture of the vet's notes and a picture of the pill bottles. She would know what they were and why Lily should take them, because Michelle had been a pharmacist. Modern technology is so convenient for transmitting information.

Michelle texted me later, don't let Lily be in pain, we trust your judgment. I sent a text back, "Let's wait and see how the pills work tonight," and promised to contact her in the morning. I came back one more time that evening to let Lily out before bedtime, and her breathing seemed a little better, maybe there was hope.

I came back the next morning to let Lily out and got her fed and give her the pills. She was happy to see me, but she always was. I picked her up and carried her outside to go the bathroom and brought her back in the house.

As I was carrying her into the house, I said to her, "Lily, you seem better this morning." She started struggling to get out of my arms. This was not like her, she always liked being carried, with her little Pug tail wagging against my arm.

Lily wanted down so I put her on the floor; I did not want to drop her. Lily walked two feet and fell on her side and fainted. I picked her up and brought her to her dog bed. She started coughing and wheezing, her sides heaving due to her breathing, and her tongue was turning dark purple.

I knew then this was Lily's way of telling me she was not getting better and the pills were not going to work, she was ready to leave her physical body.

I called the vet and described Lily's condition. It did not surprise her, and she said the pills were only a chance to keep her going until the family returned. I called Michelle, asked her to speak to the vet and let me know what she decided, even though I already knew I would be taking Lily into the clinic for the last time.

Lily would be going in later that afternoon, and I still hoped as the day went on that the pills would kick in and the family could say their goodbyes. It never gets easier and I don't want it to. I get attached to all the pets I care for and I would never change that.

I held Lily in my lap and told her I loved her and her family loved her. She brought us great pleasure, and it was an honor for me to have known her. She was a beautiful little girl and we all would miss her. I told her it was okay to let go, we understood it was her time to leave and nobody wanted her to suffer. I told her Gus would be waiting for her, that she and I could still communicate, and I gave her a kiss on the top of her head as she passed.

Again, tears were falling, but it was okay, how could I not cry, they give and give until they can give no longer.

The Clair's in this story were a combination of Claircognizance (clear knowing), because I knew Lily was at the end; and Clairempathy (clear emotion), because when Lily jumped out of my arms, I felt from her that she was ready to go. Clairempathy is an aspect of Clairsentience (clear feeling). I will go into more detail in a later chapter.

Woody

The first time I met Woody I could not believe how tall he was for a Yellow Labrador Retriever, and he was not a young dog. There was another Yellow Lab in the family also named Sam, and Sam could jump straight up in the air about two feet or more from all four feet at the same time. I have videos of him doing this.

Woody and Sam were hunting dogs and they lived for hunting. I never figured out how, but hunting dogs know when hunting season is approaching and they start to get excited. Woody and Sam's family members were Mark, Stephanie and their two boys David and Andrew, who doted on the dogs.

The first time I went to their house to do a meet-and-greet, I recognized the place. I had taken care of another family's dogs that had lived there previously named Atta Girl and Georgie. I soon was taking care of Woody and Sam every time the family was out of town.

When I would come to pet sit, I could see Woody was getting older and showing his age. In fact, in time he could no longer go on hunting trips, which was sad for a hunting dog.

It was a hot and humid Friday evening in July when I came to see Woody and Sam for the weekend. When I got there I noticed Woody was having difficulty breathing as we walked around the yard. Woody would walk a few steps then stop to catch his breath, then take a few more steps and again stop.

As we took Woody's usual route he started foaming at the mouth. I made him sit down and rest as I sat next to him, petting and talking to him. After about fifteen minutes we tried it again with the same result, the difficulty breathing and foaming, so we sat down.

This time I sat in front of him so I could look in his eyes while I talked to him. That was when I saw and knew and felt that he was ready, it was getting too hard for him to go on, but it was not my decision to make.

We got up and walked another couple feet before we had to sit down again, and the next time we got up I had to help him stand. It was time to call Stephanie.

When she answered, I told her about Woody and that it did not look good. She said he had been uncomfortable that week in the hot, humid weather, and she would talk to Mark and get back to me. I offered to call their veterinarian if that would help.

Mark called me back and said that he would be driving home. It would take about three hours. I told him I had one more dog stop and then I would come back and stay with Woody until he got there.

After I finished the dog stop, I took Woody outside for a quick bathroom break then brought him to the garage to lie on his dog bed. I sat next to him on the floor, petting him as I talked to him. Woody eventually relaxed and his breathing eased.

Mark arrived home in record time and we discussed Woody's condition. He informed me that he had talked to the vet and told me what I already knew; Woody would be going to the vet one last time the next morning.

I gave Woody a hug and a kiss, told him I loved him, was grateful for all the time we got to spend together, and it was okay to let go. I gave Mark a hug and left their house with tears streaming down my face.

I came back the next afternoon to take care of Sam, because Mark had to attend a wedding. It is always hard to return to a house with a pet no longer there, but Sam still needed support and love; after all, it was Woody who taught him to hunt and had been his companion.

Mark left me a note thanking me for staying with Woody until he got there and when he took him to the vet that morning the vet confirmed it was Woody's time. I know the veterinarian and if he does not think it is absolutely necessary, he will not end a life. I felt a little better about calling and asking Mark to drive home.

This story is another example of Cognizance (clear knowing) but at the same time Clairsentience (clear feeling), with a little Clairempathy (clear emotion). I knew it was his time but when I looked in Woody's eyes I also had the feeling and emotion along with the Clair Cognizance.

This chapter seems to suggest that all I do is cry, but there are happy times with these pets, too. I can go from a house where a pet is dying to the next house with a puppy that is delighted to see me. It is life's circle. Clients will call me and tell me they think it is time for their pet, what do I think? I always ask them, "Are you keeping your pet alive for their sake? Or are you keeping your pet alive for you?" If their pet has quit eating, drinking, and most of all has quit wagging their tail, I usually hear the same day or the next that they are taking their pet in.

I also ask them if they are going to stay with their pet until they cross over and if they are not, then I will. I offer to go with them if they prefer; it does not make it any easier but they will have my support.

I remember the first dog I helped cross over the bridge, my friend Janelle's dog Casey, a beautiful Golden Retriever. I had been cleaning house for Janelle for years and was also her pet sitter. Janelle had other dogs and cats over the years, and was very active in the local Humane Society, a board member and past president.

Casey was an aging, older dog and it was his time to go. Janelle called to say the veterinarian would be coming to her house to put Casey down and she asked if I could be there.

Of course, I would go, it would be my chance to say goodbye to Casey and comfort my friend in her grief. I did not realize how hard it would be, we were both crying, the vet even had tears in his eyes.

Often life events are released when a pet passes, especially if the family has had the pet for its entire lifetime. Janelle had recently been through a divorce and would be moving, was taking a different position at her place of work, and Casey had always been there for her. Now he was leaving.

My friend Jill called to tell me she was going to put her cat Snakehead down, an old cat that had been getting sicker. The last time I had watched her she was not doing well. Snakehead was called that because she looked like a rattlesnake on the top of her head when she was a kitten.

I agreed to go with Jill to the vet clinic and be with her while Snakehead passed over the bridge; again, not an easy thing to do, even with your friend by your side. All the emotions come out along with the sorrow. Snakehead had been with Jill a long time and was there during her divorce and the passing of family members.

It was not that Jill had never dealt with this before; she too has been a past president of the local Humane Society, has served on the board and does so currently, and has fostered pets for the Humane Society for many years.

Jill and I would bring Snakehead home to bury her. Jill's son had dug us a hole earlier that day. We had to laugh between our tears when seeing it, it was big enough for a person, and took forever to fill in all the dirt after we buried Snakehead.

It just never gets easier and that is because our pets become family members. They never criticize or complain. They will stay by your side twenty-four-seven if you let them; they always greet you with excitement and joy. Pets will sit quietly next to you, happy to be there and to lick away your tears when you are sad.

That is why I cannot stress enough the importance of being with your pets, or for someone the animal knows to join them, when it is their time. If nothing else, do so for the love they have given and their lifetime of service and devotion.

After one of my clients' pets passed they sent this poem to me with a note that read, "This is for you. Thank you very much for all you do."

If it should be that I grow frail and weak,
And pain should keep me from my sleep,
Then you must do what must be done,
For this last battle can't be won.
You will be sad, I understand.
Don't let your grief then stay your hand,
For this day, more than all the rest
Your love and friendship stands the test.
We've had so many happy years,
What is to come holds no fears.
Would you want me to suffer?
So, when that time comes, let me go.
Take me where my needs they'll tend.
But stay with me until the end,
And hold me firm and speak to me,
Until my eyes no longer see.
I know in time that you will see
The kindness that you do for me.
Although my tail its last has waved,
From pain and suffering I've been saved.
Do not grieve, it must be you
Who must decide this thing to do.
We've been so close, we two, these years,
Remember joy among your tears.
~Author Unknown

CHAPTER NINE
MAYOR DUKE

I included this story in the book because it is about a dog that silently brings a village together, makes worldwide friends and expresses the true meaning of unconditional love. Duke is a ten-year-old Great Pyrenees that lives with his owner Dave and Dave's friend Karen.

Ten years ago, Dave's dog died and he wanted another dog. Dave did his research and since he had a farm, he decided on a Great Pyrenees. Great Pyrenees dogs are a working dog with an instinct to protect everything within their domain.

Dave contacted a breeder with Great Pyrenees puppies and was told there were two females left in the litter. Dave made arrangements to meet the puppies, and when he got there the breeder said a male puppy had been returned. Dave was told he could have the male puppy for one hundred dollars. Dave was more than happy to buy the male puppy and headed back to the farm with his new dog he called Duke.

Duke grew up on the farm and was soon protecting the livestock and chickens, and at night he guarded the gardens from the deer, raccoons and skunks that would raid them. During the day, Duke, being the farm dog he was raised to be, would wander into town two miles away and visit with the villagers along the way. Little did Duke know, bigger things would come his way.

In 2014, the small village of Cormorant was trying to think of ways to raise money for their annual Cormorant days held in August. Someone came up with the idea that if you paid one dollar you could vote for an honorary mayor of Cormorant for a year. On August 6, 2014, at the age of seven, Duke the dog won the most votes and became Mayor Duke of Cormorant.

His life as a celebrity was just beginning. Word spread like wildfire and Dave was getting calls for radio interviews and newspaper articles in the New York Daily, Chicago Times, Huffington Post, Star and Tribune. They were all asking for face-time and pictures, while television stations local and far away clamored for Mayor Duke news.

Mayor Duke traveled to the Steve Harvey Show and was scheduled to be the last guest that day, but got ousted by Dr. Phil at the last minute. His segment was still taped and it went out on the internet. For the Steve Harvey Show appearance he was given a new dog house, mayor hats, bow ties, dog dishes emblazoned with the word "Mayor"; and from a local dog food company, a year's supply of dog food.

Mayor Duke has his own Facebook page and receives mail and Christmas cards from all over the world.

In January 2015 Mayor Duke went to the World Dog Awards show in Santa Monica, California, where he had been nominated for the "World Dog Award" along with other dogs. He even had his own seat on the airplane. The dog with the most votes would win the award. Mayor Duke did not win, coming from a small village and competing with world-famous dogs.

In 2015 Mayor Duke again ran for Mayor, his slogan was, "Dog of the people," and "Things might get a little hairy, but his doggy door is always open." Mayor Duke would win by a landslide.

Mayor Duke continued to raise money for local charities such as the local humane society and the county K-9 program. Mayor Duke could also be spotted in local parades during the summer, and hosted a Duke's "digging up bones" Halloween party in the fall for kids in the area and a spring fling at Easter. Mayor Duke would also go to story-time at local libraries.

Mayor Duke has a busy social life along with his farm duties.

In 2016 Mayor Duke was again elected Mayor, for his third term; he was now ten years old. During the August celebration in the village of Cormorant when the mayor is announced, there are now two to three hundred people who show up for that day of festivities and the election announcement. Not bad for a village of maybe twenty residents.

So far in 2016, Mayor Duke has been in the National Geographic kids newspaper (September 2016), the Scholastic News (November 7, 2016 Edition 4), and he travels to schools where children read his newspaper articles and have their pictures taken with him.

Mayor Duke also made the 2016 Ripley's Believe it or Not Eye Popping Oddities book and has the privilege of being one of only a few dogs ever elected mayor in America.

All this notoriety means nothing to Mayor Duke. He still guards the livestock and keeps an eye on the garden and the vegetable stand. He wanders into Cormorant Village at least once a day for a few pats on the head and make sure the local traffic is keeping the speed limit, and every Friday night he goes to the

Cormorant Pub for the prime rib, where a special doggy bag will be waiting.

Mayor Duke is a one-hundred-dollar dog that was rejected by his first owner. But that is okay because this dog has silently brought a community together that works side by side to improve their village, he has donated to local charities and causes, spends time with kids, and gives unconditional love to everyone he meets, all while he goes about the business of being a dog.

CHAPTER TEN
INTUITIVE READINGS

This chapter will illustrate what you might see, hear, sense, feel, smell, taste or know when you start activating your intuition. The readings I chronicle here were not only given to look for lost dogs but to practice my intuitive skills with clients. I have found that when working with animals, readings on the average are about fifteen to twenty minutes in duration. That is, unless I have information for the owner, which sometimes happens. Most of the time I am not present with the animal or may have never seen the animal.

That is not to say that when I am with a pet client I must conduct a session to communicate, because it happens all the time for me. In a typical reading, an animal sends single words or short sentences; they do not use paragraphs. They may also transmit a picture and a word, or a feeling and a word.

Buddy

This is what I received for Buddy when I did his reading for his pet mom: Buddy likes snow, heat, fire, warm light energy, and pine branches. I saw him chasing rabbits; a smaller ball toy; the color red appeared; I heard the song, "Love, Love, Love, All You Need is Love," by the Beatles; I was aware of a stomach sensitivity and him taking probiotics; his favorite food is chicken pops, his favorite person is his mama, and he loves her. I relayed this to Buddy's pet mom and she responded with the following.

Three years ago, Buddy was diagnosed with cancer and given months to live. She brought him home and learned Reiki for him, and took him on long walks with extra love. When he was diagnosed, his urine was red and now three years later it is normal. He loves the snow, he loves to lie under pine branches, and he sits by her side when she has a fire.

The day I did the reading he had been out chasing rabbits while on their walk. He loves chicken snacks and his favorite is chicken nuggets. The color red relates to a red flannel shirt he sleeps on that belonged to his previous owner, who has gone on. He has stomach sensitivities and is a picky eater; he will not eat anything that has made him sick. She said the song is so like her Buddy, since he loves unconditionally.

When she got off the phone with me that day she found he was excited and happy and barking; she said he hardly ever barks.

Jenny

This is the what I received from Jenny the dog when I did her reading: Jenny loves her mama; she gets nervous; I see cornstalks; I hear the words rabbit poop, rabbit poop, rabbit poop, and I see her munching on it; she is sassy and in pretty good health; she has an issue with her left back leg; I see her sitting on the couch; and she wants more walks and rides, even though they make her nervous. I also received information for her owner.

Jenny's pet mom said, "This helped me better understand Jenny's anxieties and fears." She also confirmed I had zeroed in on Jenny's personality, where she sits and her leg issue. I shared holistic treatments for Jenny's anxieties and fears, and new ways to care for her.

Mercedes

Mercedes was in spirit when I did the reading for her pet mom and this is an example of how they are still around even after they have passed.

The first message from Mercedes was a tune and I had never had this happen before. I did this reading before Buddy's, which is recounted on a previous page. The tune I heard was by the Beatles, "Let It Be, Let It Be," but the words were different. I heard, "Let It Go, Let It Go, It Will Be the Answer."

I also saw a smaller black dog, like a toy poodle, running around as fast as his little legs could carry him; a fan with three blades; a bear cage; and a woman with white hair from the other side who loved dogs.

Mercedes' pet parents said they had sold a couple of houses and still had all the belongings, and the mom was overwhelmed. She was trying to decide to keep or throw things away. Mercedes had come through loud and clear with, Let It Go, Let It Go.

The smaller black dog was a toy poodle that had passed also at an older age, crippled during its last years. She was happy to hear the dog was no longer struggling and was at peace.

The bear cage was in fact one they had purchased from a small zoo and used for a dog kennel.

The older woman with white hair and the three-bladed fan

did not make sense to her at the time, but that is ok, it might come to her later or not at all.

Bear

The first thing I saw from Bear was a mane around his neck, big and fluffy, then I heard the words lion, strength and the courage of a lion.

I also heard about food issues, chicken, eggs, something about his breathing, a rug or blanket with the color black woven in, I saw a pickup truck and heard the words 'ride in the back,' I felt a tingling in the bottom of my right foot, I heard the word chiropractor, and saw a male in the distance standing on the left side of his owner.

Bear's pet parents said he has a huge mane around his neck like a lion's mane if they let it grow out, he does have food issues and he eats eggs on top of his regular food, he rides in the back of a truck with a topper if their friend comes to get him while they are gone. Bear has a blanket with black in the design, and he has some issues with his back legs. I gave them the name of a pet chiropractor.

The male showing up could have been a couple of people, they said. When I see someone on the left side that tells me it is from the father's side, if I see a person on the right it is on the mother's side, and if I see them in the distance they have been gone for a while.

The male wanted so badly to tell me something but could not; it might have been because I did not have permission to do a reading for Bear's owners, or because it was an unresolved issue between them and the male who had passed.

I met with Bear's pet parents a day after Bear's reading and they showed me his picture. He looked like a black Lab mix, but when his hair grows out he has a mane. That is why I do not ask for a picture because in this instance my ego and brain could have taken over and said, this dog has no mane, you are wrong. I cannot stress enough the need to trust the information you receive even if it makes no sense.

Rascal

I was asked if I could do a reading on a dog named Rascal, since the owner had a concern he was in pain, I told her I would try to connect with him. This is what Rascal sent: he was old, worn-out, tired, something was wrong with his throat because I could feel it in my throat, he had teeth problems, arthritis I could feel in my body, was not hungry, liked chicken and popcorn, I saw a pine tree, a small ball other than the one he usually played with, he had shallow breathing, he is at peace, and he was sleeping on something soft with a distinctive smell.

When I called Rascal's pet mom she told me he is sixteen and four months old, he does have throat issues—a collapsed trachea. He does have bad teeth but is too old to have them fixed, and he has arthritis in his right leg. She has been giving him rice and hamburger to get him to eat. Not having much luck with that, I suggested chicken with rice boiled in chicken broth.

He loves popcorn when he finds pieces dropped on the floor, the small ball is a snowman-ball he used to chase, he does have shallow breathing, and the soft thing with a smell is probably the clothing she wears each day that he sleeps on next to the bed. Since he is blind and cannot hear his sense of smell is much stronger.

There were some end-of-life questions Rascal's mom had and I answered them.

Since this chapter was written, Rascal has passed on. I did another reading for his owner a few weeks after that so she would find peace.

Roxy

Roxy is one of my pet clients and she is a sweetheart. Her pet mom had some questions and often asks me to read Roxy.

This is what I received from Roxy: she loves riding in the car, loves lattes and coffee, I asked her what she was doing and she was watching birds, she loves the water and the pontoon boat, she needs more attention, and has a hip/back issue (I saw the word chiropractor).

When I talked to Roxy's mom this is what she said: Roxy loves car rides, her mom did not know she liked coffee lattes until she left her in the car one day for a few minutes and returned to find Roxy licking the coffee mug, she was watching the birds out the patio window, they have a puppy at the house and therefore Roxy needs more attention, and there is something wrong with the dog's back or hips since she is stumbling and her gait seems off-balance.

Charlie

Charlie is a cat I read and he is a riot. His personality is strong but sarcastic and to the point; he does not mince words.

This is the information I received from Charlie: sunshine sitting, I felt warmth, sun shed with lots of windows, peaceful, got his neck stretched, a huge castle (I received this as a picture), mice (he is proud of his hunting skills), tired, midday is the time to watch the birds, loves working with his pet mom who is awesome, and I heard the words "See ya" at the end of our conversation.

When I talked to Charlie's mom she confirmed some hits for me (hits are things that make sense to her): Charlie loves the sun; the sun shed is her own little building called the She Shed; he had seen an animal chiropractor and had an adjustment, hence the "got my neck stretched" comment; she is working with a castle on a project she is developing; mice live outside and she finds one every now and then he has killed; and she does a lot of spiritual work with him sitting by her or on her.

This chapter shows you do not need complete sentences or paragraphs to validate your communication, and that animals have a different way of looking at things than we do.

For instance, day and night to them is dark time and light time. They understand if you tell them you have to go to work and you will be home at feeding time, or dark time.

You may feel something in your body they are feeling, and they can and will pick up on your emotions.

The next chapter is about learning how to communicate with your animal.

Ruby

Ruby was a Schipperke, her pet parents were Ronda and Paul. Ruby was my first experience with this breed, and so far, my only one. Ruby had a wonderful temperament and was such a sweet dog who loved her walks when I would come to pet sit her. Ruby's fur was jet black when I first met her, and as she aged it would eventually turn to gray. *Hmm ... I know that feeling!*

As the years progressed, Ronda would ask me questions about Ruby's age, health, and end of life. Would she know when it would be *that* time? I assured her they would know. One of the last times I cared for Ruby, I knew her time was nearing. She had become deaf, her eyesight was failing and her legs were giving her problems. When I left that day, I gave Ruby a big kiss, told her how much I loved her and that she was a special girl.

Not too long thereafter, I received a call from Ronda; the time had come for them to take Ruby to the vet. Ronda was crying, I was crying, it would be a tough day for them and the weeks following.

One day I received a call from Ronda, she was having a really hard time with Ruby being gone and wanted to know if I could connect with Ruby. I told her I would see if I could get a connection, and this is what was in the connection with Ruby:

When I connected with Ruby, I saw her running around, excited and happy. She was once again a black dog, with no gray. Ruby wanted me to tell Ronda she was around her, so would she please talk to her. Ruby wanted to know where her water dish by the refrigerator went? Ruby showed me the couch and bed where she slept and that if Ronda felt fur or a lick on her face while she was sleeping, that was Ruby. She showed me downstairs, something about the two sons, a Christmas tree? Ornaments?

Ruby informed me the cat, Opal, was getting crabby and that she was still pestering the cat! Ruby told me she could see, hear and was no longer in pain. I felt a sharp pain between the eyes, one that Ruby had at the end of her life, but was now gone. Ruby wanted Ronda and Paul to know that she loved them, missed them, and had a full, wonderful life with them.

I called Ronda and gave her this information I had received. This is Ronda's response to my information:

"I found this reading to be very insightful. Only someone who knew and loved Ruby would be able to connect with her. The special water dish was the tipping point for me; Paul always hated that water dish and moved it as soon as she passed away. I have felt stirrings in my sleep. I think going downstairs had something to do with the boys, as they always had the fireplace on and Ruby's favorite place was in front of it. Plus, they were always snacking and would give Ruby treats. There was always a little Christmas tree down there at Christmastime, and we had little black dog and orange cat ornaments on it. The boys got to say goodbye to Ruby when we left for the vet that day. Opal is crabby!!! She is especially not into company and commotion and will hide under the bed for days, snarling when we try to get her to come out. Every now and then, Opal runs up and down the stairs, under the table, so that must be when Ruby is pestering her. Toward the end, December 23, Ruby's hind legs wouldn't hold her up, so I would hold her up as we took her outside. It was then we decided this was not the quality of life for Ruby. She had to be in chronic pain from the two bouts of Lyme's Disease. It's nice to know that she is pain-free, can see and hear and is running around. Ruby so loved to run and take long walks. She was such a beautiful little dog and we miss her every day. Thank you so much, Georgia for the care and love you gave to our precious Ruby. She loved you, too, and would light up when we would say 'Georgia's coming.'"

GEORGIA NAGEL

CHAPTER ELEVEN
RECLAIMING YOUR INTUITIVE SKILLS

*Take the time
to give yourself the gift
that the Universe offers.*
~Blackwolf Jones and Gina Jones

We are all born with intuition and at one time or another we quit using it, or we are persuaded not to use it, most likely by someone older than us.

For example, you might have been told when you were younger not to let the neighbors hear you say that the dog told you something or that your invisible friends are not real, so you eventually stopped using your intuition. It's put away in the closet of your brain. It might make an appearance every now and then and you wonder, "How did I know that?" or think, "My gut told me to do this," and back in the closet it goes.

I am here to tell you, go right ahead, I give you permission, give yourself permission: use your intuition. Bring it out of the closet and become familiar with it, like a comfortable sweater or a favorite pair of jeans. You have the ability, but just like a muscle that is not used, it can become weak. You need to strengthen it with practice.

Some of you pet parents are probably communicating with your pets and you don't even realize it. For instance, do you know when your pet is not feeling well or should go to the vet? Or perhaps you can sense that they don't like something or it makes them nervous? You think about taking them for a ride or walk and when you get home they are all excited and ready to go. You are communicating with your pet by your intuition.

I will share what I used to do, what I thought I had to do (believe me, it was quite the process), and what I do now, which is much simpler.

When I first started out I knew I had some ability because the events of the previous chapters validated what I was receiving from the pets. I wondered if I could carry on a conversation with a pet and ask questions that they would answer.

I remember the first time I decided to try to connect with a pet for a client. I went to the farthest corner of the basement in my house, almost into the closet, and closed the blinds to make the room pitch-black. I assumed I had to be in complete darkness even though I closed my eyes, in order to shut out the busy, logical part of my brain. I knew I could not communicate with a pet if my mind was racing a hundred miles an hour.

I also had stones with me (I have always been a rock person), although I was not sure why at the time, along with crystals, and a pen and paper.

I sat on the floor, took a few deep breaths, and grounded

11 | RECLAIMING YOUR INTUITIVE SKILLS

myself by imagining roots growing from the bottom of my feet reaching deep into the earth. I tried to quiet my mind and clear it, easier said than done if you have a busy mind.

I would think of the dog's full name, tell the dog who I was and ask permission to connect with them.

The first couple times I tried this I received answers that were too logical, too complete, so I knew my brain was still active.

I kept practicing and soon learned to quiet my brain, but then my ego stepped in and told me what I was receiving was not right, and who was I to think I could connect with a pet?

I wrestled with my ego until I figured out how to silence it. To this day ego stills pops in every now and then, but I ask ego to go for a nice long walk while I do my communicating.

When I received information, I put off calling the client, fearing what they would think of me. Would they say I was out of my mind? My ego was trying to protect me and keep me safe. It told me there was no need to change, things were just fine the way they were, I had no reason to step out of the box.

The only reason I kept trying was that pet owners would call and ask for my assistance in locating their lost pets. My love for animals was stronger than my fear of being wrong and hearing a negative opinion of me.

I would suggest that I try to connect with their pet to see if I could get any information from them. Not once did anyone say, "Are you joking?" Maybe it was because their pet, a part of their family, was missing and they were willing to try anything.

As I began to do more and more communicating with pets, I found I did not need an hour to prep the room and myself, and I did not need to do it in the middle of the night when it was quiet and peaceful and my mind was less active.

I still sometimes go to the room in the basement just to get out of my office and away from all the electronics, so I can receive a clearer signal.

I also found I was not taking a whole pile of rocks with me, just pen and paper.

In the earlier days, I also used a pendulum to double-check what I received, which was another example of ego taking over to make sure I was correct.

Learn to trust what you receive and trust yourself.

Today when I do a pet reading with a pet, I ask for an Archangel to assist me, whichever one I am drawn to at that time. I also ask for the help of any ascended masters, like St Francis, or an ancestor you were close to.

I have a lot of animals that have passed around me so I often ask my power animals, along with my two dogs that have crossed, Shooz and Midnite, to assist me.

I then say a short prayer "for the highest good of all those involved and to be guided to the information that is needed. Thank you and so it is."

I tap my heart to get my direct connection to spirit, quiet my mind and then say the animal's full name, ask to connect with them, and begin the questions.

Most of the time you will be given their permission, but that does not mean they want to talk to you right at that moment. You can always try again at a later time.

When I talk about getting or receiving, I can be shown a picture, I can hear a word or a sentence, I might feel an emotion or a pain in my body, I might know something I did not before, and some people get a taste in their mouth, or a smell.

I wrote this chapter out by hand on paper first, and when I thought I was finished, I could smell burning sage, and the next thing I knew I had more to write. When again I thought I was done, I smelled burning sage and had more to write; this happened three times before I finally quit for the night.

I have a spirit guide that hangs around and is a Native American Chief. He was guiding me to put more information in this chapter. I know you might think this sounds crazy, but this is not the first time it has happened, he appears quite regularly when I speak or write.

My point is you might smell a perfume someone close to you wore, or a food someone loved. Just be aware of the signs.

As you exercise your intuitive muscle you may start to develop more than one way of receiving information. That is great, but don't feel bad if you don't.

Practice will make it stronger.

There is no right or wrong, it is all about what works for you.

When you start out asking a pet questions, make them simple, like: Do you have a favorite toy? What is your favorite treat or food? How old are you?

The owner might have a specific question they want answered, and you can ask that at any time in your conversation.

Do not expect long, drawn-out paragraphs, answers usually come in a word or short direct sentences, or a picture.

While conversing you may find that some pets have a fun personality or a sarcastic sense of humor; they might be a joker or even take over the session.

When successful, you can contact the owner and tell them what you have received during your reading.

This is where pen and paper came in handy; as you get information, write it down so you do not forget anything. I scribble it down, because when I started out my eyes were shut and I did not want to open them because I did not want to break the connection I had established.

When you speak to the owner, give them one word or sentence at a time so they can digest it and determine if it means anything to them. This also gives them a chance to validate what you have been given. Do not be disappointed if it is not all a hit (hits are answers that make sense to the owner), the meaning may become clear later.

It is wonderful when your messages are confirmed, you are excited, but at the same time your logical brain and ego might say, "Are you kidding?" You may have to tell your ego to take a hike.

When you start out you may want to use oracle cards, tarot cards (I personally do not work with a regular tarot deck; it does not resonate with me).

I still work with my power animal cards, energy oracle deck, ascended masters deck, Shaman's oracle deck, nature-speak deck and animal-wise tarot. You can find these on the internet, research them and see what appeals to you.

You can also use affirmation cards. These decks not only help you work through events in your life but you can use them to help others. Affirmation cards raise your vibration level with positive thoughts.

I also have two pendulums, one brass and one a crystal. The recommendation is for beginners to use the brass pendulums, since they are easier to work with. Pendulums have been used for years in government, science, by healers, and for personal guidance. Some people are frightened by them, thinking they are objects of magic or voodoo.

A pendulum is an extension of you when you hold it; it is part of your body, which causes it to swing. When using a pendulum, ask which way it will swing for the answer yes, and which way for no. For me, a yes is a swing back and forth vertically, while a no is a swing horizontally. Your direction may be just the opposite, so ask to be shown. It is similar to muscle testing, in that your body gives you the answers.

All the above you can do yourself, but I recommend getting together with a friend or friends to play intuitive games to strengthen that muscle. Make it a fun afternoon or evening, remembering it is just practice.

You can pair up and pick who is to be the receiver and who will be the sender. Now choose a color and tell the receiver the color and send a picture of something that color, add an emotion to it and say the word silently.

For example, the color is yellow, and you, the sender, imagine the sun, think the word sun, feel the warmth as you project it, and picture a big bright yellow orb. I suggest you say the word silently, feel the emotion, and picture the sun, because the person you are transmitting this to may only have one way to get it, maybe only by the picture, or the word, or feeling the warmth.

Now it is time for the receiver to tell the sender what they got and time for the sender to validate it. You can switch places and repeat the process

When you are with your friends, bring pictures of your pets that are living (at this time you probably do not want to start conducting mediumship, which is communicating with pets or people who have crossed over).

Pair up and trade pictures and hold the picture they have given you; do you feel anything? Can you sense their personality? How about their favorite toy, food, or treat? As you look at the picture and hold it, write down everything that comes to you. When you are both finished, share this with each other. You will be surprised by how much you get right, more than you expected.

If you have a friend who owns horses, spend an afternoon communicating with them, because horses are the easiest to understand for most people.

Just remember to ask for permission, whether it is an animal or person you wish to read. I even ask for approval when I take pictures of pets.

How you receive may be different than how I receive and that is okay, we are all unique and the universe works in a way best-suited to your understanding.

I suggest you start journaling. Keep a pen and paper by your bed so when things come to you at night you can jot them down. Messages come to me in the night. I write them down, and in the morning, I do not remember much, but find the information amazing.

You could also try something called automatic writing. Close your eyes, ask yourself a question you want answered and start scribbling on the paper. Keep the pen moving, and when you get a word, write it down, and then go back to scribbling.

You can set a timer for a minute or two or three if you want when you first start out. Just set your intention and start moving the pen until something comes to you.

I have done this in a notebook for automatic writing and I

date the pages. I am surprised when I go back to read what I wrote a month earlier; sometimes it made no sense at that time but makes perfect sense now.

All these exercises can help you build your intuitive muscle. The more you use it, the stronger your intuition gets. You were born with intuition; it has always been with you, so start using it again.

Don't do like I did for years, buying books, taking classes, searching and hoping, thinking it is more difficult than it appears, thinking only certain people have this ability and the rest of us have to learn it. I was wrong; it is not difficult, quit searching and just do it.

1. Believe in yourself
2. Leave your ego at the door and quiet your busy mind
3. Listen, listen and listen again, they are communicating with you
4. Receive the information and trust it, don't second-guess yourself or try to make sense of it
5. Thank everyone involved

The information I receive today comes much faster, and sometimes when I am with the pet it comes immediately, just as if we are carrying on a conversation.

It took a lot of years of not knowing what I was doing for me to learn how to understand it and discern what was happening. I hope I have helped you understand that things do not have to be as complicated as we like to make them, and intuition is a gift we were born with.

Enjoy communicating with your pet or pets. I believe in you and your abilities, so just have fun. You got this!!!!

GEORGIA NAGEL

CHAPTER TWELVE
TOOLS

I do not know if you believe in psychic sense or mediumship, but you came into this world with intuition. Call it what you like, gut instinct or gut feeling, but these are all names for the same ability and you have used it since the day you were born.

You can expand your intuitive senses or you can ignore them and hardly ever use them. The people who use them and develop them become psychics, mediums or communicators. Which are you going to be?

In this chapter I have described some of the Clairs, your Chakras and Helpers, in case you want to go further with this, even if it is just to connect with your pets.

CLAIRS

These are psychic senses or an awareness that helps you connect to information that seems beyond the normal way of receiving it. Whether you believe in God, angels, ancestors, spirit guides, power animals or the universe, these are your connections and psychic sense helps you understand information they send.

Clairs are your gifts or the abilities you use to receive knowledge that can be of use in your everyday life. Everyone has their own views on this; some people believe there are no Clairs, only intuition, others believe that there are five Clairs, and others believe there are more. Do some research to learn what feels right for you and use your intuition.

Clairvoyance

Clairvoyance (clear seeing) is when you can see a vision or a picture, but not with your eyes. You might see it in your mind, or in your third eye, which is located in the center of your forehead, above your eyes and between your eyebrows.

You might see outlines, figures, shadows, and some may be clear and distinct while others may not.

You might see things that have happened in the past or may be happening now or will happen in the future.

The dictionary defines Clairvoyance as: the power or faculty of discerning objects not present to the senses, the ability to perceive matters beyond the range of ordinary perception. A person with this ability is a clairvoyant, people with this ability are sometimes asked to help find missing persons or pets.

Clairaudience

Clairaudience (clear hearing) is the ability to hear things without using your ears. Some people may hear songs, lyrics, or poems, even just a verse of a song or a couple words from that song. You may also hear words, names, noises, animal noises, or sentences.

The dictionary defines clairaudience as: power or faculty of hearing something not present to the ear but as regarded as having objective reality. Someone with this ability may be called clairaudient.

Clairsentience

Clairsentience (clear feeling or sensing) is something you feel, like a gut instinct; you may feel it in your stomach.

An example may be that you took a different way home than you usually do, or you get the feeling you are being watched and you look around to see someone staring at you.

Of all the psychic senses this is probably the most common, but also the most important. This is the one that may warn you about a dangerous decision, place, event or person. It is the gut feeling that ends up being true; or when you may meet someone, something about them just doesn't sit well with you. If you listen to this sense you may save yourself much pain and trouble.

The dictionary defines clairsentience as perception of what is not normally perceptible. If you have this ability you are called a clairsentient, and most mediums have this ability.

Claircognizance

Claircognizance (clear knowing) is the feeling that you know something to be true, but you do not know how you know it, you just do. It seems to appear out of the blue or just pops into your head.

The dictionary defines claircognizance as the ability to acquire knowledge without knowing how or why. A person with this ability is a claircognizant, and this sense is one that almost everyone uses in their daily life.

Clairempathy

Clairempathy (clear emotion) is the ability to take on the emotions or feelings of others. If you have this psychic sense it is important to learn how to ground and protect yourself from the feelings or emotions of others.

With this ability, you can be standing next to someone and get the feeling they are sad or happy without even talking to them. Have you ever come up to someone you know and asked them what's wrong? You had an immediate awareness when you saw them.

The dictionary defines clairempathy as an ability to tune in to the emotional experience of a person, place or animal. A person with this ability is called an empath or clairempathic.

Clairgustance

Clairgustance (clear tasting) is the ability to taste something without having anything in the mouth. You may be doing a reading and you start to taste pickles; maybe a person who has passed away loved pickles and that is the connection they are using to get a message to you so you know who is coming through.

Often when clairgustance is present, you are also working with another Clair.

The dictionary defines clairgustance as the ability to taste a substance without putting anything in one's mouth. It is claimed that those who possess this ability are able to perceive the essence of a substance from the spiritual realm through taste. If you have this ability you have a clairgustory sense.

Clairalience

Clairalience (clear smelling) is the ability to smell cologne, perfume, a certain food, or flowers that remind them of a loved one that has passed on. The smell may come across very strong or faint.

The dictionary defines clairalience as acquiring psychic knowledge by means of smelling. If you have this ability, you have a clairalient sense.

Clairtangency

Clairtangency (clear touch) is holding or touching an object and picking up the energy from that item, it is also called psychometry. For example, when holding a ring, you can gain knowledge about the person who owned that ring.

This sense works with other psychic senses.

The dictionary defines clairtangency as divination of facts concerning an object or its owner through contact with or proximity to the object.

CHAKRAS

Chakras are "spinning energy" centers in your body that help you to maintain your physical, mental, emotional and spiritual balance. Your chakras can aid you in your work with intuition.

There are seven chakras in the body. I am going to give a

quick overview of each chakra so you have basic knowledge for each one and what they do. I would suggest you do further research on the chakra system.

Root Chakra

The first chakra is the root chakra. The root chakra is located between your anus and the genitals. The Sanskrit meaning is root or support system.

The root chakra is associated with the color red and affiliated with your sense of smell.

Your root chakra relates to your survival and physical needs.

Sacral Chakra

The sacral chakra is the second chakra in your body and it is located between your navel and genitals, in the lower abdomen area. The Sanskrit meaning is sweetness.

The color orange is associated with the sacral chakra and it affiliated with the sense of taste.

Your sacral chakra relates to your emotional balance and your sexuality.

Solar Plexus Chakra

The third chakra is the solar plexus chakra and it is located between your navel and the base of your sternum. The Sanskrit meaning is lustrous gem.

The solar plexus chakra is associated with the color yellow and affiliated with your sense of sight.

Your solar plexus chakra relates to your personal power and self-will.

Heart Chakra

The fourth chakra is the heart chakra and is located in the center of your chest. The Sanskrit meaning is unstruck.

The color associated with the heart chakra is green and this chakra is affiliated with the sense of touch.

Your heart chakra relates to your relationships and love.

Throat Chakra

The fifth chakra is the throat chakra and is located at the base of your neck. The Sanskrit meaning is purification.

The color blue is associated with the throat chakra and this chakra is affiliated with the sense of hearing.

Your throat chakra relates to your communication and self-expression.

Third Eye Chakra

The sixth chakra is the third eye chakra located above and between your eyebrows. The Sanskrit meaning is to perceive, to know.

Indigo is the color associated with the third eye chakra and it is affiliated with the sixth sense.

Your third eye chakra relates to your intuition and wisdom.

Crown Chakra

The seventh chakra is the crown chakra located on the top of your head. The Sanskrit meaning is "thousand-fold."

Violet is the color associated with the crown chakra and it is affiliated with your sense of "beyond self."

Your crown chakra relates to your spirituality.

I have found that if I have a blockage in one of my chakras and the energy is not flowing, I need to have a massage or a Reiki session to clear those impediments.

There are many associations with each chakra, I only touched on a few, but they include: glandular connections, body parts, ruling planets, zodiac signs, incense and oils, crystals, animals, physical dysfunctions, sacramental associations, foods, development, age, and life lessons.

I would encourage you to expand your knowledge on chakras. A book I like and refer to often is, "The Book of Chakra Healing," by Liz Simpson. This offers information, charts, and exercises, and is easy to read.

You can also take Reiki classes and become a Reiki master. If your body is in alignment your intuitive awareness will be magnified.

I discussed pendulums, tarot, oracle, and affirmation cards in the previous chapter. I also work with essential oils on myself and while working with animals. Be aware that cats are very sensitive to essential oils and cannot process them, so read up on oils and cats before you use them on or near a cat.

If you do not have an animal of your own, you can always ask a local shelter or rescue group if you can practice your intuitive abilities with their animals.

Grounding

I should say a few words on grounding or protecting yourself. I do this so I will not take on the emotions, feelings, or energy of the person or animal I am reading.

To ground myself I take a few deep breaths then envision a bright white light or beam coming through the top of my head, my crown chakra, and moving through my body until it reaches my feet. I visualize roots growing out of my feet and into mother earth, where she recycles the white light and it again fills my body.

You could also ask Archangel Michael to surround you in his blue bubble of protection. And you can say a prayer.

HELPERS

You can ask any of your helpers to help with your intuitive skills. Choose any helpers that resonate with you, be they spirit guides, power animals, guardian angels, ancestors, ascended masters, or the archangels.

Archangel Michael is the angel of protection, guidance, strength, direction, self-esteem, courage, life's purpose and releasing fear.

Archangel Jophiel is the angel that helps to manifest beauty into our lives, helps with artists, designers and brings hope and joy to you.

Archangel Chamuel is the angel of unconditional love, and helps with careers, finding lost items and world peace.

Archangel Gabriel is the angel of communication and helps you speak your truth.

Archangel Raphael is the angel of healing mental, physical, and emotional and spiritual areas of your life, along with guidance and support for healers, clairvoyants and finding lost pets.

Archangel Uriel is the angel of illuminating situations, prophetic information, writing, clarity and new ideas.

Archangel Zadkiel is the angel of forgiveness, mercy, benevolence, emotional healing and memory.

Archangel Ariel is the angel of the earth and helps with healing of animals.

St. Francis is the patron saint of animals and environment.

There are many more angels and saints; I suggest you do further reading on them. Sunny Dawn Johnston has a great book called, *"Invoking the Archangels,"* and Doreen Virtue has written wonderful books on angels as well.

CHAPTER THIRTEEN
SHALL WE TRY?

Now that you have a number of tools and the information given throughout the book on how animal communication started out for me, I am guided to add another story to illustrate this concept. I keep hearing, "do an example, do an example," so here is a sample of what I do for a reading with an animal or a person.

This is only an example of how I do a general reading. You may find other ways that work for you or that are more natural for you. Go with what you are guided to do, there is no wrong way if it is for the highest good of all involved.

Always ask for permission, whether it is an animal or a person, their privacy deserves respect.

I recommend that you do not sit across from your pet and stare at them; it will only make them uncomfortable and nervous, and they may even leave the room.

I would also recommend communicating with a friend's pet you don't know well. If you're reading your own pet and you get some hits, your logical side, your ego, might step up and insist you knew that already, you did not receive anything new. The ego is difficult to get past, since it wants to keep you protected and logical.

If reading a friend's pet, you can work from your own home, and if you need a visual you can ask them to send you a picture.

Okay, so now you have chosen a pet you are going to connect with and maybe have a picture. The next step is to grab a pen and paper (make sure the pen works; nothing is more frustrating than when information is flowing to you and the pen has no ink!).

Make yourself comfortable in an area where you can quiet your mind, the less background noise the better. I also try to be in a room with very few electronics, and leave your phone in another room.

Now that you're settled, you may want to ground yourself. When I ground myself, I use the technique described earlier: I imagine a white light coming into the top of my head, going through my body and down to my feet, where I imagine roots growing out of my feet and deep into the earth. The white light goes from my feet into the earth to recycle it and send it back up through my body.

At this time, you can say a prayer if you feel guided. I usually ask for guidance from my guides and helpers, to receive information for the highest good of all involved, and thank them.

I also tap my heart center a couple times to affirm my intention of unconditional love for all involved.

Start by saying the pet's full name. I then tell them my name and ask for their permission to communicate with them.

You now may begin asking your questions. Make them simple at first so that the answers can be given in only one or two words.

An example would be, "Do you have a favorite food?" Let's

say the pet answered back, "Chicken." Some of you might hear the word chicken, some might see a picture of a chicken in your mind, some might taste chicken in your mouth, and some of you might get two of the three above. It depends on which of the Clair's are more dominant for you.

Ask as many questions as you want, but with animals you may find some of them are talkative and others not so much, you might find a joker or one with a sarcastic attitude, and they will all have unique personalities.

When asking a pet about a health issue, you might be shown an area of their body, or hear a word, or you might feel something in your own body. You can tell the owner that you feel there may be an area of concern that needs to be checked. Just remember, you are not a veterinarian and you cannot make a diagnosis; you may suggest they take their pet to a vet for an examination and tests.

When you are receiving information, write down exactly what you receive, and do not put your twist on it to make sense of what seems strange or not logical, it's not about you.

When you feel your conversation is done, thank the pet, your guides and helpers.

Now comes the exciting part for most beginners, you can call up your friend and share what you have received and see if they can give you any hits. Do not be discouraged if they cannot validate all of it, it may come to them later.

If you are communicating with an animal that has passed, do the same as above, but I also ask for the assistance of Archangel Michael for protection from any negative entities seen or unseen. I do not need any negativity present around me.

When communicating with pets that have passed you might

get a strong feeling or emotion besides the things we discussed when working with a pet that is living.

You might also hear from other pets that are no longer here and every now and then a person might also show up with a message for their loved one. If that happens, I always ask the person I am doing the reading for if they want to hear from anyone besides their pet. Let them make the choice of whom they want to hear from.

In all the readings I have done, I have never had a negative experience but I do not go into a reading expecting one. I give each reading with love and intentions for the best interest and highest good of all involved.

Do not be discouraged if you receive nothing the first few times. It is very hard to shut down the chatter of your brain; your logical side wants to show up and interfere. Keep exercising your intuitive muscle, be still and listen.

CHAPTER FOURTEEN
IN CLOSING

As I come to the end of my book, there are a few things I would like to touch on that I have learned from my eighteen years of pet-sitting and animal communication. The following words pretty much sum it up.

A Pet's Ten Commandments

1. My life is likely to last 10-15 years, any separation from you is likely painful.
2. Give me time to understand what you want of me.
3. Place your trust in me; it is crucial for my well-being.
4. Don't be angry with me for long and don't lock me up as punishment. You have your work, your friends, your entertainment, I only have you.
5. Talk to me. Even if I don't understand your words, I understand your voice.
6. Be aware that however you treat me, I will never forget it.

7. Before you hit me, before you strike me, remember that I could hurt you and yet, I choose not to bite you.

8. Before you scold me for being lazy or uncooperative, ask yourself if something might be bothering me. Perhaps I'm not getting the right food, have been in the sun too long, or my heart might be getting old or weak.

9. Please take care of me when I grow old. You too will grow old.

10. On the ultimate difficult journey, go with me, please. Never say you can't bear to watch. Don't make me face this alone. Everything is easier for me when you are there, because I love you so.

Take a moment today to thank God for your pets. Enjoy and take good care of them. Life would be a much duller, less joyful experience without them. We do not have to wait for heaven to be surrounded by hope, love and joyfulness. It is here on earth and has four legs.
~ Author Unknown

I hope you now understand animal communication better and that it is not a thing to do or to master. It comes from listening to another from the place of love, from the intention of the highest good for all involved.

I also hope this book has brought you insight on how important the relationship is between you and your pets. It is a bond of unconditional love from them to you.

I ask you to give that unconditional love back to them and to others. Let's raise our vibration of love for everything on this earth, and we will become a brighter light for the world to see. So, go now and listen to those who speak silently.

GEORGIA NAGEL

PET GALLERY

MY BOYS: SHOOZ and MIDNIGHT (CHAPTER ONE)

SHOOZ (CHAPTER ONE)    MIDNITE (CHAPTER ONE)

SAMZAK (CHAPTER TWO)

RUSSEL (CHAPTER THREE) 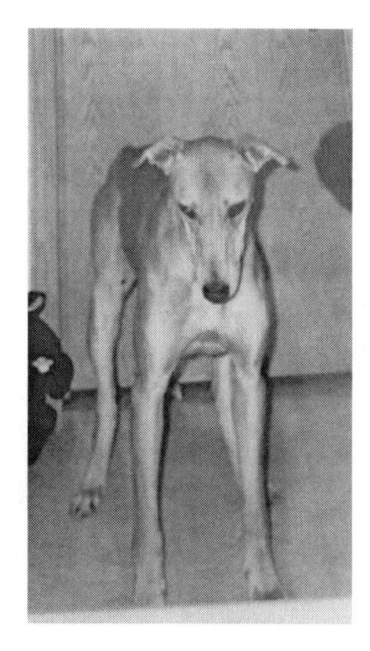   KNUCKLES (CHAPTER THREE)

Mi'Lady (CHAPTER THREE)

YETI (CHAPTER THREE)

GINGER (CHAPTER THREE)

CHARLIE AND SOPHIE (CHAPTER 4)

PET GALLERY

BUSTER (CHAPTER FOUR)

BAILEY (CHAPTER FOUR)

BOOMER (CHAPTER FOUR)

FLASH (CHAPTER FOUR)    SOPHIE (CHAPTER FOUR)

PET GALLERY

PJ (CHAPTER FIVE)

MAIZEY (CHAPTER FIVE)

MEG (CHAPTER FIVE)    ROSIE (CHAPTER FIVE)

MAHARSHI (CHAPTER SIX) 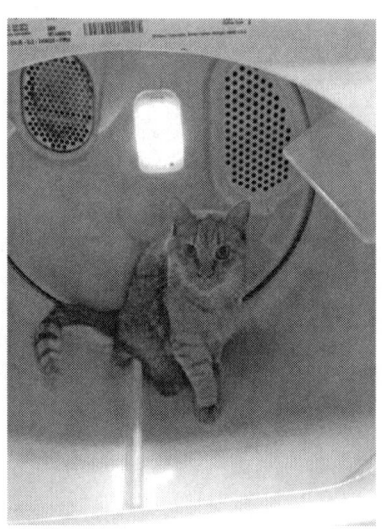   TIGGER (CHAPTER SIX)

PET GALLERY

BOOMER (CHAPTER SIX)    GIZZY (CHAPTER SIX)

MARIUS (CHAPTER SIX)

DAISY (CHAPTER SEVEN)

DOTTY (CHAPTER SEVEN)

PET GALLERY

IZZY (CHAPTER SEVEN)

ANGEL (CHAPTER SEVEN)

COOKIE (CHAPTER SEVEN)

BETTY (CHAPTER SEVEN)

GRACIE (CHAPTER EIGHT)

PET GALLERY

LILY (CHAPTER EIGHT)

WOODY (CHAPTER EIGHT)

MAYOR DUKE (CHAPTER NINE)

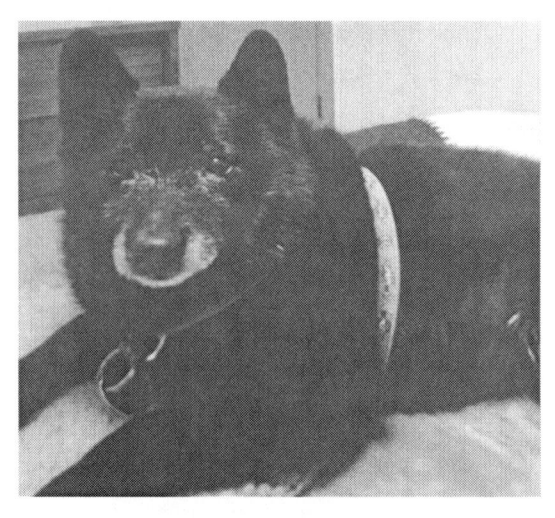

RUBY (CHAPTER 10)

ABOUT THE AUTHOR

Georgia possesses a great love for the earth, nature and animals. She resonates with the vibration and connection she receives when working with them. Her life journey has been intertwined with animals, nature and earth medicine. She believes we are all interconnected, earth, animals and people, and if we share the unconditional love given to us by the first two and apply it to all those we encounter, we will together shine a brighter light.

She writes about the unconditional love of animals in a number-one best-selling book with multi-authors, titled, "The Peacemakers."

Georgia is an Animal Communicator, having discovered her ability through her own two dogs who have now passed on but continue to work with her every day.

Her pet-sitting business has also brought many animals to her who have helped strengthen her intuitive abilities over the past eighteen years. She uses her intuition, knowledge of essential oils and Reiki to help her pet clients with the issues or problems they face. Along the way, the owners also receive benefits themselves during the process of interacting with their pets.

Along with being an Animal Communicator she is also a

certified Mind, Body and Spirit Practitioner, Invoking the Archangels instructor, a Shaman Practitioner, and an ordained minister, she performs ceremonies for people, animals and the earth.

Georgia loves her work and practices her gifts and abilities from the place of unconditional love for the highest good of all involved.

ACKNOWLEDGMENTS

I am thankful to have the support of Jeff, my loving better half, who encourages me to do my thing, as he calls it; my mother Donna, for her concern; my dad George, looking down from above; my brother David, and his sense of humor; my sister Michelle, to whom I sent copies of each completed chapter for safe-keeping; my nieces and nephews who never failed to ask, when will your book be finished; my grandma Bess, at 99 years young, asks about the animals every time she sees me and all my friends. They may not understand fully what I do, but encourage and support me always.

I acknowledge Eloise Irvine, who is well into her nineties but loves listening to my stories whenever I stop by to see her and made me promise to write them all down in a book.

I would like to acknowledge Sunny Dawn Johnston, Shanda Trofe, Melissa Corter, Jodie Harvala and Jeanne Troge, my mentors and teachers, all beautiful, spiritual women who over the years have helped me grow and expand into the person I am on this destined journey, with their patience and love.

Last but not least, thank you to my tribe, all the pets and their owners who have trusted and believed in me to take care of these precious fur babies. You may not realize it but you have helped me to understand my life's calling.

A special thank you to all who have picked up this book and will spread the UNCONDITIONAL LOVE to everyone they encounter, whether human or animal. In doing so, your light will shine brighter.

Love, Georgia

TESTIMONIALS

"Georgia is someone I'm proud to call one of my besties. She is loyal to a fault, loves her friends unconditionally, and is always honest—so painfully it hurts. If you ask her opinion you will get a truthful answer, like it or not. When you talk to her she listens. She is focused on you and what you are saying, a rare quality. Her compassion for animals is unparalleled. I know no one like her. She is one in a million and I am honored to call her my friend."

—Jill Mickelson

"Georgia's reading for my dog Jenny helped me to better understand her and thus be able to ease her anxiety and fear. Georgia zeroed in on my dog's personality, describing it to a tee; this was amazing as she did the reading long distance and had never met Jenny.

Georgia also guided me to holistic means to support and care for Jenny.

I loved the way Georgia quickly tuned in and conversed with my dog on a higher, compassionate level.

Georgia also did a reading for me. It felt very authentic and organic. Georgia's insight provided much helpful information on the direction my life is taking and on issues I struggle with.

She had a direct line to spirit evidenced by the way the reading flowed and the knowledge that was given. I would highly recommend her services to anyone. I felt supported and uplifted when the reading was over."

—Kim Ness

"From pet lover, to caregiver, to adviser—Georgia wears all the hats. She has taken care of our dogs in many capacities over the past eight years.

Georgia has offered suggestions to improve their health and well-being, taken care of them when we were out of town, and cried with us when they left this earth.

Georgia is a wonderful resource on a variety of needs for our family and we could not have found a kinder and more dedicated person to care for the furry loved ones in our absence.

We have been comforted and nurtured by the love and care that Georgia has provided our dogs over the past eight years.

While we were on vacation, our dog had a seizure, and Georgia slept on the floor with him and gave him Pedialyte with a turkey baster to keep him hydrated so he could live long enough for us to return home.

Georgia's dedication has gone beyond our expectations and she has offered much knowledge, love and support with our dogs. She is their other family!"

—Sherri Komrosky

"I was blessed to have Georgia do a reading for my dog Buddy.

Almost three years ago I took Buddy to a vet and learned he had cancer that could not be treated, with only a few months to live. It crushed me as he was my boy.

I was given Buddy from a friend's parents who had to move off their farm, so he was around five or six when he came to me.

When his cancer was diagnosed, I began doing anything I could to help him, and he never seemed to have pain but his urine was red. I started him on vitamins and took him on regular walks, assuring him he was loved.

Later that year I learned Reiki and started practicing this healing art on him and his urine returned to normal.

I wanted Georgia to do a reading on Buddy to see if there was anything else that would help. Georgia's reading was awesome and it showed me that Buddy feels good and knows he is loved.

Georgia saw beautiful warm light around Buddy and felt great energy. I believe that is true, and part of that light is from his previous owner shining down his love. He passed away one year after I got Buddy.

Georgia said Buddy told her he liked snow and he does like snow, he gets very warm in the summer, and since he has grown older he doesn't like the cold but he likes the snow.

Georgia also said she saw pine branches and he likes to lie under the pines in the summer when it is hot. After the reading today I found pine needles in Buddy's fur—pretty cool.

Georgia said his favorite food was chicken pops, that's what Buddy called them, and yes, he loves his chicken snacks, and really loves chicken nuggets.

Georgia said she saw a red cloth, so I asked my friend if he had anything red when he was younger. She said Buddy slept on a red flannel shirt that belonged to his previous owner, the man looking down from heaven. That was awesome to discover.

The words Buddy kept repeating to Georgia were, Love, Love, Love, to the tune by the Beatles, and that is so much like my Buddy. We share an unconditional bond with each other, the best ever.

Georgia said Buddy has stomach sensitivities and that is true. I wondered why he was always picky about his food, but Buddy knows what he can and cannot eat.

I love that when Georgia asked Buddy about me, he said I was his FAVORITE!!

I loved hearing about my Buddy and it made me realize again how much animals know and feel. I always understood that but the reading told me Buddy is alright and meant to be in my life.

After the reading, I went out to Buddy and he was excited and barking; he doesn't bark much unless he is happy so that was cool to see.

—Dena Hanson

"Georgia's reading for my dog Gabby gave me insight into what she was feeling and what was in her heart.

Georgia used essential oils to release the grief Gabby was feeling and to fill her with joy. Gabby received peace as well as healing.

Georgia advised me on what would make Gabby feel better and how I could manage certain behaviors.

Georgia's read on Gabby also gave me peace and clarity, and a greater understanding of myself."

—Mary Beth Ellegaard

"I have had pets my entire life. This summer we moved from West Fargo to Detroit Lakes and that is when we met Georgia. Georgia was asked to come and let my dogs out twice a day.

It soon became obvious to me that she did much more in the few short months I have known her. Georgia has given me a better understanding of my pets' needs, wants, fears, desires and expectations.

Georgia recently helped my Ole English bulldog pass. She was a great comfort to me, my family and our other two Bullies. I could not have done this without her.

Georgia may advertise as a pet-sitter, but she will become a loved and valued part of your family."

—Susan K. Trauman

WORK WITH GEORGIA

I love to work with nature and the creatures of this earth. If you would like to continue this journey with me, below are ways I may be able to assist you.

ANIMAL READINGS

- Animal Communication Classes
- Learning To Work with Your Intuition Classes
- Learning to work with oracle cards using nature, trees, flowers and animal cards

CEREMONIES

- Weddings
- Blessings on a new home, new property, and at earth and garden ceremonies
- Animals: Blessings on a new pet, at end of life, for pet funeral and pet celebrations of life

If any of these services are of interest to you or you have any questions, you may contact me at:

WWW.GEORGIANAGEL.COM

WWW.WHOLETSYOURDOGSOUT.NET

MY BLOG: "THE GEORGIA CONNECTION"

**OR EMAIL ME AT
GEORGIANAGEL.INFO@GMAIL.COM**